Philip Mattera holds a graduate degree in economics from the New School for Social Research and is a business journalist for magazines such as *The Nation*.

GP85 00310

Philip Mattera

Off the books

The Rise of the Underground Economy

St. Martin's Press

Published in the United States in 1985 by
St. Martin's Press, 175 Fifth Avenue,
New York, NY 10010 (all rights reserved)

Cover designed by Clive Challis A.Gr.R

Phototypeset by A.K.M. Associates (U.K.) Ltd,
Ajmal House, Hayes Road, Southall

Printed in Great Britain by
Guernsey Press, Guernsey C.I.

ISBN 0-312-58206-4

Contents

Acknowledgements

What started out as the subject of a reporting assignment ended up as a major influence on my view of the world over the past six years. A number of people have helped me refine that view. Special thanks to the following people, who took the trouble to read and comment on various chapters of this book: Randall Dodd, John Downing, Joanna Hadjicostandi, Richard McGahey, Vladimir Padunov and Nancy Condee. Conversations over the years with George Caffentzis, Paolo Carpignano, Bruno Cartosio, Silvia Federici, Ferruccio Gambino, Christian Marazzi and Bruno Ramirez have been of great value.

Thanks to Pete Ayrton of Pluto Press for getting me to gather my dispersed thoughts into book form. Melissa Sutherland did a superb job on the word processor.

A special debt of gratitude is owed my family, especially my parents and grandparents, for their enthusiastic support every step of the way. 'Acknowledgement' is much too weak a word for what I want to say to my life's companion, Donna Demac. Her endless encouragement and support prevented this book from joining the roster of unrealized projects.

1. Going underground – an introduction

Until a few years ago, the term 'underground' had, aside from its literal meaning, mainly a political connotation. It was used to describe individuals or groups that were opposed to an established order and had to carry out their activities in a clandestine way. The Underground Railroad was a system of co-operation among nineteenth-century opponents of slavery in the US by which fugitive slaves were secretly helped to reach the north or Canada. Dissidents in the Soviet Union disseminate their books and journals by means of underground publishing houses. Guerrilla fighters in situations ranging from the Resistance during the Second World War to contemporary Northern Ireland and Poland have gone underground to avoid detection and arrest.

In the late 1970s the word was attached to a new kind of defiant behavior. Growing numbers of people had begun participating in economic activity – working, buying, selling – that was outside the view and outside the control of government. Seeking to evade taxes and avoid compliance with state regulation, many otherwise law-abiding citizens had entered into an underground economy.

A long list of adjectives has been applied to this area of activity: informal, irregular, black, hidden, shadow, parallel, and so forth. What all the terms refer to are transactions that are 'other', that do not conform with the rules set down by the state in its role as overseer of the economy. The rapid growth of illegal economic activities that transgress state provisions other than the criminal code is remarkable. This economy is underground due to the violation of tax laws, licensing requirements, labor standards, and other regulations that governments have established since the end of the age of laissez-faire.

The substantial volume of media coverage that has been devoted to the underground economy in the past half dozen or so years has tended to trivialize the phenomenon, portraying it as little more than a popular sport of diddling the taxman. Simple cheating is certainly part of it, and the very willingness of such large portions of the population to put themselves at risk with the law is of no small significance. Yet the increasing frequency with which people are forced or choose to work 'off the books' is a symptom of a more fundamental change that is occurring in economies throughout the world. One of the major developments of the twentieth century is being reversed: many people are no longer looking to governments and labor unions to provide a broad measure of social and economic security. Almost everyone is still working for a living, but their employment is less and less covered by a system of guarantees. For a variety of reasons, the body of protections that decades of liberal democratic (in the US) and social democratic or socialist (in Europe) policies had created is rapidly contracting.

Some of this change is due to the crises of the state and the union movement themselves; these trends have been analyzed by a wide range of commentators. What has received far less attention has been the change in the way people go about earning a living today. With the weakening of the institutions that had been overseeing relations and setting standards in the workplace, earning a living has taken on a much greater degree of uncertainty and instability. Work has become increasingly irregular in character, so much so that the traditional categories of economic activity no longer seem adequate. With people piecing together incomes from a variety of regular and unofficial jobs, government benefits and other sources, it is much harder to describe anyone as simply 'employed', 'unemployed', or 'not in the labor force'.

Many of these new forms of work take place off the books and thus contribute to the underground economy. By escaping the scrutiny of government, the participants in this unofficial realm subvert the state's direct regulatory function and, by evading taxes, impair those policies subsidized by public revenues. Freed from that control and the regulations that go along with it, economic activities once again take on greater risk and instability. For those with capital, this may be a welcome development, permitting unfettered pursuit of that sacred practice known as entrepreneurship. For that much larger section of the population that depends on the sale of its labor to survive, this brave new world may be less appealing.

The unprotected employment offered by the underground economy is not all of a kind. In fact, it can be said that there are two very different sectors of the underground in terms of the working conditions and financial rewards experienced by the participants. On the one hand, there has been a resurgence of the sort of precarious labor that permits the worst forms of exploitation. Sweatshops, child labor, outwork and other supposedly anachronistic working arrangements have been appearing with alarming frequency in many of the 'advanced' industrial countries.

The workers forced into this kind of informal activity tend to be women, blacks and people of immigrant background. Relegated to the lowest rungs of the labor market, these groups are most susceptible to rogue businessmen whose enterprises pay little heed to labor laws. In a time of shrinking employment and reduced government benefits, these workers have had to take whatever jobs were available, and in recent years those positions have more frequently been in the underground economy.

For another group of people, toiling off the books is an entirely different experience. Skilled workers can moonlight to earn additional (untaxed) income while their primary occupation provides basic economic security. These workers, who tend to be white and male, are also often in a position to abandon their regular job and establish an underground business. The lack of taxes and government regulation help raise the chances of success.

In terms of class structure, the informal economy mirrors the conventional one. There are both capitalists and workers in the underground, and the labor force is segmented into a hierarchy based to a large extent on divisions of sex and race. This suggests that the distribution of underground income among workers is roughly parallel to society at large. It appears that the rate of profit of underground firms is higher than that of their 'legitimate' counterparts, but the clandestine nature of this and all other informal activity precludes statistical confirmation.

Even in its most exploitative forms, underground labor appeals to many workers because of its flexibility. The ability to work on and off in irregular schedules often fits in best with the new patterns of family and personal life. Informal labor also provides an alternative to the mainstream economy and its frequent crises. In periods of economic instability, many people have found underground activity the surest route to survival.

In its more benign aspects, the informal economy can be seen as liberating for some people. Working in less rigid ways and no longer depending on large corporations and the state, these underground participants achieve a greater measure of social autonomy. A number of futurologists have emphasized this point while overlooking those people for whom life in the underground economy is more of a nightmare than a utopia.

The underground economy, then, is a contradictory and politically confusing development. This does not mean, however, that it can be dismissed as a mere media invention or minor social phenomenon. Informal economic activity is assuming a role of increasing importance in the new shape of economic life throughout much of the world.

The forms of informality

It is worth spelling out in more detail what is meant by the underground or informal economy. There are several senses in which transactions in this realm are different from conventional economic ones.

First of all, they are *unregulated*. By keeping their activities secret from the government, participants in the underground economy are able to escape compliance with the multitude of laws that have arisen to regulate exchanges between employers and employees as well as between other buyers and sellers of commodities. Off-the-books labor is not covered by minimum wage levels, maximum hours, prohibitions on moonlighting, job security, occupational health standards, and anti-discrimination rules. Nor does the underground worker receive benefits such as paid holidays, sick leave, health insurance, and pensions that have been established by governments and unions for workers in the regular economy. Underground entrepreneurs can also ignore laws relating to consumer and environmental protection as well as licensing requirements.

Second, these transactions are *untaxed*. No income tax is withheld from the wages of workers and no contributions are made to social security programs. It is here that the whole practice takes on the form of collusion between labor and management to cheat the government. The political significance of employees and employers seeing themselves as having a common interest in conspiring against the state (in its fiscal role) could be profound. For now it is enough to note that this is happening as both parties in the private sector seek to increase their net income. Employers gain by avoiding payroll taxes and reducing labor costs. Businesses which are not completely underground but which seek to evade taxes by understating the volume of their sales can do this more effectively when their official labor costs are reduced as well. In any case, the loss of revenue to government is massive.

Third, these transactions are *unmeasured*. Because underground activities are not reported to the government, they are not directly reflected in official statistics on the economy. Along with a shortfall in tax compliance, the state is faced with a shortcoming in its ability to estimate accurately the volume of productive activity. Some analysts of the underground economy claim that much of the economic malaise of the past decade has been nothing more than a statistical illusion caused by the large amount of production and employment that now takes place off the books. They claim that the true state of the economy – that is, including underground activities – is healthier (and vastly larger) than anyone had thought.

The most common and most important form of informal activity is working off the books. This phrase is the best available to express the combined characteristics just outlined. While most commentators in the US and the UK have emphasized the non-payment of taxes and the exclusion from official figures on labor force activity, it is probably the absence of regulation that is the key characteristic of the informal economy. It is symptomatic of the eroding status of waged workers in the advanced industrial countries. Unregulated labor that is entirely off the books is but the extreme form of a change in the terms of employment affecting increasing numbers of people who work for a living.

In the course of the crises of the past dozen years, business has sought and to a great extent has succeeded in regaining control over the wage relationship. The decently-paid and secure jobs that so many unions traded their political souls for are steadily becoming extinct. At the same time, many of the government benefits that were supposed to tide people over difficult times are being dismantled. Regular jobs, when they are available, are increasingly precarious in character: lower paying, without benefits, temporary rather than permanent, part-time rather than full-time. Underground labor represents the sinking of these conditions below the minimum standards established by law. Yet once the opportunities for tax evasion and illegitimate collecting of government benefits are added in, working off the books in some cases may seem more attractive.

It is unlikely that many people participate exclusively in the informal economy. Some kind of legitimate activity is necessary if for no other reason than to have a 'cover' when inquisitive tax investigators start prying into one's affairs. An underground occupation may be most attractive as a supplement to rather than a substitute for a regular job or other activity. Working off the books is thus often seen among people in the following situations:

Moonlighting from a regular job

In some European countries such as France the prohibitions against having a second occupation on the side are so strict that moonlighting is almost universally done off the books. In the US and Britain, where no such limitations have existed, a fair amount of moonlighting has long been carried out on the books. But during the difficult times of the past decade, larger numbers of people in these countries have also turned to second occupations and pursued them underground.

The officially unemployed

When layoffs were infrequent and short in duration, spells of unemployment were often received as welcome breaks in the monotony of working life. Today, for large portions of the labor force in many countries, being on the dole is a permanent state of affairs. With the extension of unemployment and the restriction of unemployment benefits, the jobless are frequently engaged in part-time and temporary work that must be done off the books to avoid endangering one's eligibility for benefits.

Those officially not in the labor force
These include a variety of people who need additional income but who cannot take official jobs without running the risk of losing essential welfare benefits. Examples are retired workers collecting pensions, injured workers collecting disability benefits, students receiving education benefits, and housewives (in Europe) whose husbands receive family allowance payments.

In all these cases, the motivations for working off the books include a combination of the need for additional income and the requirement that the money be earned in circumstances other than a full-time, permanent, official job. It is essential that the activity be untaxed (so that the maximum cash benefit can be gained) and unreported (both to help in evading tax and to protect one's official activity, whether it be a job that bans moonlighting or collecting a government benefit that precludes other income). What is also important is the flexibility and irregularity of the informal activity. Because it is often being done in addition to a regular activity, there simply is not enough time or too great a risk for it to be carried out as a full-time, permanent job.

Off-the-books work is invariably fragmented and erratic. When the labor is done for a wage, it will often be performed only for a few hours a day or a couple of days a week. But a great deal of work done in the underground is paid in a lump sum rather than on an hourly basis, and it is common for the labor to be done by someone working as a freelancer or independent contractor.

While some underground participants are moonlighting from a regular occupation, others may conduct their primary activity partially or entirely off the books. Among professionals and skilled workers this often occurs by means of *unofficial barter*. In recent years it has become common for such people to exchange services with one another without the use of cash. The lawyer represents the carpenter in court, and the latter repays the former by building some cabinets. The whole process seems innocent enough, but from the point of view of tax authorities, both parties are guilty of failing to report income that was taxable even though it was received in kind rather than in cash. The extreme difficulty faced by revenue officials in enforcing tax laws relating to such exchanges has made barter one of the most popular segments of the underground economy. In the US several hundred barter clubs have sprung up in recent years. These organizations bring together people with different services to offer, and allow them to accumulate credits (for services rendered) that can be used to purchase the services of anyone else in the club. Because the participants in the organization (and not the club) are the ones required to report these transactions to the Internal Revenue Service, the vast majority of the exchanges never end up on tax returns.

Proprietors of regular businesses also participate in the underground economy to the extent that they deliberately conceal some of their receipts from the tax collectors. In the US it is not unusual for retail enterprises that operate in cash to keep two sets of books: one with artificially low revenues, which will be used for tax purposes, and another that allows the owner to keep track of how much he is really making from the business. The removal of unrecorded (in the first set of books, that is) cash receipts from a business is known as *skimming*, and in the US it is practised everywhere from the corner store to casinos in Las Vegas.

When business is not transacted in cash, the techniques of understating taxable income are more complicated. In order to prevent glaring discrepancies that would be detected in a tax audit, the dishonest proprietor must understate his purchases of raw materials and labor as well as his sales. This requires collusion with suppliers and customers as well as employees. The search for an effective deterrent against evasion led Britain and other European countries to adopt value-added tax (VAT) systems. However, many smaller enterprises still manage to beat the system.

There are some individuals in regular occupations who are also in a position to understate their actual income and thereby reduce their tax bill. These are people whose income is not received in the form of a wage and thus is not subjected to what is known in the US as withholding of tax and in the UK as pay-as-you-earn deductions. Freelance writers, artists, musicians, consultants and others with the status of independent contractors get paid their fees in full and are supposed to declare all that income to the tax authorities voluntarily and pay the appropriate levy on the total amount. In the US individual payments of $600 or more are supposed to be reported by the payer to the Internal Revenue Service, which could then check to see that that money was reported by the recipient. In general, however, the opportunities for evasion are substantial. That also used to be the case for waiters and waitresses and others who received tip income in cash. Only a small percentage of that money got declared on tax returns until 1982, when the Internal Revenue Service cracked down. Restaurant workers were then required to pay withholding taxes on an assumed level of tips calculated from reports that proprietors had to file.

The universe of economic activities that is separate from participation in regular, on-the-books, tax-law abiding enterprises is quite large. Because of the lack of agreement on the limits of what constitutes the underground economy, writers on the subject have been free to pick and choose among a vast range of human endeavors. If the terms 'informal' and 'underground' are to have any force, they cannot be catch-all categories that take in everything left over after official, mainstream activity is defined. For that reason, it will be useful to review some of the forms of activity that have at times been included in the underground economy but which in this book are considered as separate phenomena.

General tax evasion

Fiscal authorities may be deprived of revenues in a variety of ways. Some of them are technically legal, and in such cases the customary term is tax avoidance rather than evasion. Wealthy individuals and corporations are skilled in this practice, which is aided by tax codes biased in favor of capital accumulation. The majority of the population approaches the tax-minimization effort in a different way. They may faithfully report all of their income to the authorities but then overstate business expenses and other deductible items that reduce the amount of income subject to tax.

In the US, this form of cheating is made possible by the complexity of the tax code and the myriad expenses that an individual may deduct from taxable income. The Internal Revenue Service relies on a system in which taxpayers generally compute their own tax bill, which may involve an additional payment or a refund from what has been withheld from wages, or, in the case of the self-employed, from what has been paid in installments of estimated tax. Only a small fraction of returns are extensively checked, and many people choose to cheat and gamble that they will not get caught. Losing this sort of lottery means being picked out for an audit and being compelled to account for all of one's deductions. In most cases some expenses are disallowed (even when they were not fictitious), and the taxpayer must make an additional payment, including penalties and interest.

The overstating of deductible expenses is illegal and punishable but in no real sense is it underground. There is no economic activity that is being concealed. All that is happening is that the character of a previous (and overt) transaction is being disguised; a personal expense is misrepresented as a business or otherwise deductible expense.

The hidden economy, or the fiddle

In the UK, with its less malleable tax code and more limited involvement of the taxpayer in determining what is owed, more attention has been paid to practices within regular businesses by which managers and workers receive unofficial forms of income – a process known as fiddling.

It is common in the UK as well as other countries for business executives to fiddle by means of their expense accounts. This occurs when one puts personal expenses on the account or even, arguably, when one spends more than is necessary (say, in ordering a costly bottle of wine during lunch with a client) in a legitimate business expenditure.

For waged workers, the analogous practice is that of receiving income in kind or in cash on the job that is not included in pay-as-you-earn calculations. In some cases goods and services are directly distributed by the employer, ranging from materials related to work (such as overalls or gloves) to things given out to generate good will (such as a ham at Christmas). In other instances, the goods and services may be taken with the tacit approval of the boss; for example, unofficial perks such as coal taken home by miners or petty and innocent pilfering such as the office supplies taken home by clerical workers or personal calls made on the company phone. Employers often tolerate this activity as long as it remains within limits.

What is less acceptable to bosses is when workers take it upon themselves to appropriate significant amounts of goods and services. British writers such as Jason Ditton, Stuart Henry and

Gerald Mars (whose work will be discussed in a later chapter) have produced a body of fascinating empirical research on the sophisticated ways in which workers rip off their employers. Yet what these authors call the hidden economy is different from underground activity. Fiddles are essentially the misappropriation of resources used in the overt operation of a regular business enterprise. Those resources are declared by the company as part of the cost of doing business. Unlike participants in the underground economy proper, the fiddler is not concealing productive activity but rather is diverting goods and services from a regular firm into personal consumption and thereby reducing the efficiency of that firm.

It is true that the fiddler is receiving a kind of unreported and untaxed income, but it is not income derived from a clandestine productive activity. Fiddling, in other words, cheats the state of its share (in tax) of existing business output, while the underground economy deprives the state of its share (in tax) of additional activity.

The criminal economy

Underground economic activities are illegal to the extent that they violate tax laws and other government regulations. But they are distinct from outright criminal activities such as drug dealing, prostitution, illegal gambling and other 'productive' underworld pursuits, as well as lawbreaking activities such as theft that involve the forcible redistribution of existing wealth.

Criminal activities are unusual in that the income derived from them is taxable (though rarely is such a levy collected) yet is not included in official calculations of gross national product. Part of the reason for the latter is that data on such activities are obviously quite difficult to collect; but there is also a moral reason for the exclusion: most economists do not consider illegal commodities as 'goods' that should be included with their legitimate counterparts in a calculation of a nation's economic achievement. Nevertheless, many analysts of the underground lump together legal and illegal unreported income.

The decision in this book to consider crime as distinct from the underground economy is less a moral than an analytical one. Illegal profit-making activities have taken place as long as there have been laws. The growth of the informal economy, on the other hand, is an aspect of the contemporary crisis of capitalism. It is significant that large numbers of people have resorted to economic activities that have some of the same attributes as criminal pursuits, but that does not mean that crime and the underground economy are one and the same. Nevertheless, it is admittedly difficult to determine where the underground leaves off and where the underworld begins. This problem will be taken up at greater length in chapter 5.

The social economy

Some analysts of the crisis of the past dozen years have detected an increasing tendency on the part of people, especially those of the working class, to satisfy more of their economic needs without resorting to transactions with regular businesses. But unlike underground activities, which involve exchanges that are off the books, this sort of informal economy avoids the use of cash and barter. Instead, goods and services are exchanged among friends, neighbors and relatives in nonmarket activities that have been termed the social economy. Reciprocity is far from absent but it is not expressed in strict monetary terms. What is involved might instead be called an informal network by which favors are regularly given and received.

It is difficult to know how to approach these activities from tax-collection and GNP-calculation points of view, but it seems apparent that such trading of favors does not belong in a definition of the underground economy. There is nothing particularly secret about such behavior, nor is it in any way new. It may, however, have some sociological significance in terms of the various ways people survive hard times.

The household economy

Before the discovery of the underground economy, housework was the most hotly debated form of economic activity outside regular market enterprises. Feminists convincingly argued that the importance of such unwaged activity to the reproduction of capitalism had long been ignored by most conventional economists; they pointed to, among other things, the exclusion of housework from estimates of GNP. While this debate is important, it is separate from the question of the underground economy.

That part of the household economy that some observers have linked to the growth of informal activity is the realm known as do-it-yourself. These analysts have found evidence that another response of working-class families to the crisis has been to replace, wherever possible, the purchase of goods and services with the practice of meeting those needs themselves. To some extent this means a return to earlier forms of housework (say, baking a cake instead of buying one) but it also includes efforts to perform chores that the family had previously hired someone to do. Again, this is something that may have sociological significance, but it is not a part of underground economic activity.

The practice of calling underground production and all these related activities 'economies' is something of a misnomer. Some of the ones just discussed are not, strictly speaking, economic at all. And even the underground economy is not an economy separate from the capitalist one that remains entrenched in the countries of North America and Europe. Just as traditional criminal activities are distinct from but linked (albeit in complicated ways) to the mainstream economy, so are informal pursuits carried out in systems still dominated by corporations and other institutions that are very much on the books.

The aim of this book is to show that what goes on in the underground is far from unrelated to what is happening in the larger economy. One may prefer to use the term informal or underground *sector* rather than economy; what is mistaken is to claim that the underground realm has a logic of its own. It will be argued instead that the phenomenon is inextricably tied to the crisis of the economy at large. Some chapters will look at how this is the case with regard to the transformation of the labor market, the new forms of criminal activity, and the crisis of the state.

The extent of underground activity has been the subject of heated debate. Chapter 4 reviews the attempts that have been made to measure underground gross national product, and the Appendix estimates the size of the informal labor force.

The growth of the underground economy has presented a challenge to governments of all political persuasions. Activity which is off the books undermines the attempts of liberal and social-democratic regimes to solve economic problems through state intervention. The conservatives who have come to power in the US and Britain may be more sympathetic to unregulated and untaxed business activities, but they are bothered by the fact that underground transactions violate the law and aggravate the fiscal problems of government. Chapter 6 is devoted to the ambivalent relationship of American and British politicians to the informal economy, and the same theme arises in the chapters on Italy, the third world, and the Soviet Union and Eastern Europe.

The chapter on the third world considers how the informal sector fits into the patterns of development and underdevelopment. It also shows how the global integration of production includes use of underground activity and thereby helps to create conditions in the first and third worlds that are increasingly similar to one another.

This is followed by a look at countries that have planned economies but also experience unplanned and unregulated production and exchange at a level comparable to or perhaps surpassing that of the west. Although the capitalist and so-called socialist economies have different underlying problems, in both cases underground activity is the strategy adopted by large parts of the population to improve their material conditions.

Throughout the chapters there is an unavoidable tension between seeing the phenomenon of the underground economy as a heightening of the exploitation of labor and seeing it as a collection of clever ways people have found to beat systems that are oppressive or inefficient. There is no way to resolve this ambiguity: the balance between the pernicious and potentially liberating aspects of the underground economy will be a central focus of struggle in the years to come.

2. The fragmentation of work

> Ah, the work underground. Everybody knows it exists, but it is like a bit of mercury, you can't put your fingers on it.[1]

This is the way an official of the US Bureau of Labor Statistics responded to a reporter's query when the media became interested in the underground economy in 1978. Despite the large volume of writing on the subject, there is much about the phenomenon that remains elusive.

The confusion has been heightened by the tendency of most analysts to depict the underground as an anomaly. The absence of taxation and the lack of adherence to government and union standards are thought to make it a realm unto itself. Whether painted in glowing or dismal terms, working off the books is usually considered to have little relationship to what goes on in the regular economy.

Here a different point of view will be presented. The underground economy will be seen as part of the transformation that is overtaking the western industrial world. The social and economic arrangement on which postwar growth was based is rapidly disintegrating, and is being replaced by a new state of affairs characterized by austerity and greater insecurity. The old promise of good and steady jobs for all, decent fringe benefits and adequate social services are no longer part of the scenario. The new script features declining living standards brought about by an unstable economy and laissez-faire state policies.

In the language of economics, this amounts to a situation of dualism. One part of the labor force is holding onto higher paid, guaranteed jobs. This group includes those industrial workers whose special skills fit into the factory of the future as well as certain categories of white-collar workers and professionals.

A second, larger part of the workforce finds itself on a downward slide. Made superfluous by technological change in large-scale industry or trapped in depressed regions, these workers face a much more difficult time earning a living. Joined by young people recently out of school, they make up what in some areas appears as a permanent surplus labor population.

The work that this second group tends towards is irregular, poorly paying, insecure and non-union. The employers are small and unstable firms that could go out of business at virtually a moment's notice. In the worst cases, the jobs are only available in sweatshops, which flagrantly violate union norms.

It is not uncommon for this kind of marginal labor to be done off the books. Fly-by-night entrepreneurs like to keep their existence unknown to the government, so that they are better able to ignore labor laws and other regulations as well as evade taxes. The workers themselves may prefer to keep the job unofficial in order not to jeopardize their eligibility for government benefits. Underground work, then, is a particular form of marginal labor; it is precarious activity taken past certain legal barriers. The informal economy is a part of the erosion of the security of employment.

If the changes that are going on amount to a reversal of the upward social mobility that characterized the earlier postwar era, then it makes sense to look for signs of the future among those sectors of the population which were largely bypassed in that 'age of affluence'. The poor who inhabit the lower rungs of the labor market hierarchy continued to experience precarious working conditions while the better organized and more powerful sectors of the labor force achieved somewhat better terms. It is among the less powerful that we can find the origins of the underground economy.

Work and hustling

By the early 1960s an extraordinary arrogance had permeated the thinking of western social scientists. Under the banner of the post-industrial society, sociologists announced the end of conflicts and the arrival of mass consensus. Economists proclaimed that the business cycle had been tamed and only fine-tuning of the economy was necessary to achieve permanent prosperity. At the same time, the population, mainly black, that was conveniently overlooked in this celebration of well-being was simmering.

In the US, the civil rights movement of the 1950s raised political and economic expectations that were not being met by the liberal policies of the Kennedy and Johnson administrations. Starting a few months after Kennedy's assassination, the frustration boiled over and one city after another exploded in ghetto rebellions: Harlem in 1964, the Watts section of Los Angeles in 1965 and dozens of other places in 1967 and 1968. Leaders of business and government were alarmed and desperately sought answers as to why blacks were so angry and what could be done to appease them. President Johnson appointed a commission on civil disorders to supply some of those answers. One of the more controversial conclusions reached by the commission, which was headed by Governor Otto Kerner of Illinois, was that poverty and unemployment in black communities were among the main causes of urban unrest.[2]

Thirteen years later, the pattern was repeated in Britain. After young blacks (as well as whites) fought police in Brixton in 1981, the Thatcher government asked Lord Scarman to analyze what had happened. Like Kerner he found that economic deprivation was an important element in the conditions which gave rise to the revolt.[3] In both countries the riot reports prompted widespread debate on the best ways to deal with the volatile inner cities.

Whereas conservatives preferred to rely on a stronger police presence to keep the poor in line, the liberal and social-democratic approach was to improve labor market opportunities for ghetto residents. In the US, the latter concern prompted a wave of studies of employment conditions, which questioned the traditional tenets of labor economics.

According to conventional theory, all workers start out on an essentially equal footing in the labor market; employment levels are strictly a matter of supply and demand; wage rates are simply a reflection of the marginal productivity of individual workers; and labor force participation is a function of the trade-off between work and leisure: in short, a perfectly rational and equitable state of affairs. The studies of labor conditions in the ghetto brought to light a less attractive picture. Unemployment rates were persistently high, and for those who found work it was invariably low-paying, unstable, unskilled, low in status and lacking in opportunities for advancement. Some economists began arguing that ghetto residents were trapped in a separate or secondary labor market that perpetuated their poverty.[4]

Radical economists went further, speaking of a segmented rather than simply a dual labor market structure. It was by stratifying labor force participants, so the argument went, that capital kept workers divided and therefore that much less powerful.[5]

What was most important in this new labor market analysis was the recognition of the complicated ways poor people obtained the means of survival. First of all, work for them did not mean a full-time, permanent, decently-paying job that in addition helped to determine one's social identity. Rather it was an irregular, intermittent activity that provided income on an unpredictable basis. One did not have *a* job; one had lots of jobs that lasted for varying lengths of time and brought in varying amounts of money. This relationship to waged labor was quite different from the relative security experienced by white (and some non-white) workers in better-paying, often unionized jobs.

Another important discovery of the period was that irregular 'legitimate' employment was often combined with other irregular activity on the part of many inner-city inhabitants. While it may now seem obvious that impoverished people may be inclined to break the law to obtain the means of survival, traditional criminology assumed the existence of a distinct criminal class whose members rarely if ever had anything to do with the regular labor market.

What studies of the ghetto economy revealed was that activities included under the rubric of 'hustling' represented the intermingling of the precarious work of the secondary labor market and illegal enterprises, and that this was the predominant form of activity of most poor people, aside from those (mainly women with young children) who depended on payments from the state. In a 1972 study that shocked many academics with its calm discussion of these matters, Stanley Friedlander stated:

> Hustling often is an economically and socially rewarding way of life for many people. Moreover, it contributes to a quasi-

stable social existence in slum areas capable of exploding
from the tremendous economic and social tensions generated
by poverty, uncertainty, hunger, disease and insecurity.[6]

As with the underground economy today, the discussion of
hustling was often imprecise in its definitions, particularly with
regard to the legal status of the activities. Some of the components
were clearly criminal in a traditional, common-law sense; above
all, robbery. But others, such as illegal gambling and sale of drugs,
were economic activities that just did not happen to have the
approval of the government. Often, legitimate business and illegal
activity were combined, as when a shop served as a front for a
criminal enterprise. Here the term 'hustling' is used to indicate
ghetto economic activities that took place under precarious
conditions – whether legal or illegal, on or off the books.

Hustling is similar to underground labor in the diversity of
remuneration it provided to participants. For some, the combination of pursuits did little to raise them out of a miserable
economic condition. They were as exploited and as impoverished
when they were running numbers as when they were doing a lousy
minimum-wage job for a 'legitimate' employer. Yet there were
others, such as successful dope dealers, who did quite well in the
world of hustling.

Friedlander's research on ghetto areas in US cities also showed
that the places with the greatest amount of reported property
crime in 1966 had the *lowest* ghetto unemployment rates. The old
idea that unemployment caused crime was stood on its head:
instead, it turned out that the availability of criminal activity and
hustling served to keep down the numbers of those officially
jobless.

Marginality outside the ghetto

As long as the mainstream economy remained fairly sound, the
phenomena of hustling and what the economists called under-
employment (irregular work at low rates of pay) were considered
characteristic only of the poor. US liberal reformers saw these as
part of a syndrome that kept the non-white population margina-
lized, and they argued that government 'manpower development'

programs were needed to bring these people into the primary economy. Despite enormous sums of money spent by the federal government on such efforts, not much has changed in the inner cities of the US.

With the onset of the economic crisis of the mid-1970s, other groups of the population found themselves experiencing some of the same conditions. This emerged first and most clearly among young people. Youth unemployment reached astounding levels for both whites and blacks, and the work that was available was often menial and poorly paying. This, combined with petty criminal pursuits such as marijuana dealing, gave them patterns of activity that began to look much like the hustling of the ghetto. Labor market experts and government officials began to worry about the consequences of having a new generation of workers grow up without the discipline of a regular job. The *Wall Street Journal* nervously inquired in 1977:

> Even if the problem is in large part a certain shiftlessness among the nation's youth, as some cynics suggest, that is not a matter to be taken lightly. Should it be dealt with by tightening up on unemployment compensation standards? Does it imply a serious breakdown in secondary education? Does it suggest a vast subculture of youthful 'hustling' and crime that obviates the need for honest labor?[7]

What it did suggest was that unemployed hustling youths represented another vanguard with regard to changes in labor conditions. As the 1970s proceeded, more sectors of the labor force found themselves facing similar conditions. Insecure jobs, irregular employment, low pay and poor benefits – all the characteristics of precarious labor in the ghetto – edged up the labor market hierarchy, becoming the way of life for an even larger number of workers.

By the 1980s, the old debates over whether workers in the advanced industrial countries had become part of the middle class seemed quite inappropriate. In their place emerged discussion of the 'vanishing middle'.[8] The rapid disappearance of better jobs in industry and their replacement with much poorer positions, or often none at all, suggested that a process of social polarization was taking place. Large numbers of people were driven closer to poverty, while a few found themselves better off than before.

Fragmentation of the job

Along with the rise of structural unemployment over the past decade, the labor market in most western industrial countries has been transformed by the rapid migration of women into the paid labor force. Whether working out of economic need or personal desire or a combination of the two, many of the women moving from unwaged housework to waged employment did not want full-time, permanent work. Business, which at the same time was expanding the sort of service work that required irregular schedules, saw an opportunity to tap a new source of cheap labor. This lower-paying employment soon became the fastest growing portion of the labor market.

Part-time work served the needs both of female workers and their employers. The women were able to fit paid work into schedules that usually still included household and childcare responsibilities. But their bosses made them pay for the privilege: in the majority of cases part-time workers received lower hourly wages than their full-time counterparts and reduced fringe benefits or none at all.[9]

Closely related to the growth of voluntary part-time work in permanent jobs has been the spread of temporary employment, both full- and part-time. The temporary work industry operates by putting workers on its payrolls and renting them out at a substantial profit to companies needing extra labor for varying lengths of time. In periods of economic uncertainty – which now means the forseeable future – employers are much slower to put people on the regular payroll when business starts to pick up, and this means increasing use of temps.[10]

Just as temps can start and stop working as they please, so can employers using the service get rid of the additional personnel whenever they wish. Like many part-timers, temporary workers have to suffer lower wages and the absence of almost all fringe benefits and some legal protections. In some instances, temps are used steadily by a single company for long periods of time but are never offered a permanent job and the benefits and better wages that go along with it.

The different statuses of workers give management greater control in dealing with employees and create divisions among workers (in addition to those of race, sex, etc.) that can hinder solidarity. One of the founders of the temporary employment industry in the US seemed to be giving business a prescription for such control when he advised managers to hire only 75 per cent full-time permanent workers, along with 15 per cent full-and part-time temps, and 10 per cent part-time permanent employees.[11]

In some cases the subcontracting of labor takes place directly with the workers, rather than through the mediation of a temporary agency. In recent years business has been making increasing use of independent contractors and freelancers for work that might have previously been done by people on staff. In the UK there were precedents for this in the construction industry, where workers had long been paid on a 'lump' rather than an hourly wage basis.[12] This transformation of wage labor into a form of self-employment is sometimes eagerly sought by the participants, because of the obvious tax-evasion opportunities created, once taxes are no longer deducted at the source by the Internal Revenue Service or Inland Revenue.

In other cases the 'independence' of independent contractors and the 'freedom' of freelancers are far from real. The supposedly autonomous status is simply an excuse for employers to deny regular employment and decent rates of pay. This precarious status has even extended into the professional ranks. For example, increasing numbers of university teachers in the US have been compelled to work without permanent positions. These 'gypsy scholars' move from college to college with short-term appointments that offer no possibility of tenure; or worse, they are hired by an institution to teach a single course (at miserable pay) and have to commute between several campuses to put together a living.[13]

What all these new forms of work represent is an increasing fragmentation of the conditions of employment. The full-time, permanent, decently-paying job with benefits is less and less the norm. In its quest for greater flexibility in the use of labor and for lower costs, business has opened the door to a variety of unorthodox work arrangements.

What, then, is the relationship of all this to the underground economy? The general point is that informal activity did not emerge in a vacuum. It arose at precisely the time that the traditional labor market for the majority of workers was undergoing an upheaval. A crisis in industry was making large numbers of organized workers economically superfluous or else changing their jobs into much more uncertain and less remunerative situations. Simultaneously, women were coming into the paid labor force and finding themselves working in irregular schedules and often for substandard pay and benefits. The meaning of employment was dramatically changing in the regular economy, becoming more and more precarious and unrewarding.

It is true that the increasingly precarious nature of many regular jobs may have made it unnecessary for businesses seeking flexibility to hire people off the books. But this is more the case for large companies, which in any event would probably find it difficult to engage in any informal activity. Smaller enterprises, on the other hand, are likely to see going off the books as the logical next step in the modification of traditional working conditions. It can also reinforce the firm's own under-reporting of income by helping to make the whole operation seem smaller to a tax investigator. In addition, as flexible as conditions may get in regular jobs, employers still must conform with basic government labor standards. Having someone work off the books may be the only way to ensure complete managerial discretion over the conditions of employment.

The erosion of work and income in the regular economy has also put pressure on people to find additional sources of cash in order to survive. A side activity off the books has become an essential supplement to inadequate income from the regular economy for some people and an essential supplement to inadequate unemployment or social security benefits for others.

'Cop-out' from the work ethic

It is not accurate to depict the migration of people into the underground economy solely as a method of survival in difficult economic times. Just as women entering the paid labor force over the past two decades have been willing to take lower-status jobs for the sake of flexibility, so have many people looked to the underground economy for possibilities of working in ways that fit in better with personal needs and desires. The need to earn money is greater than ever, yet the widespread yearning for a different relationship to work that started in the 1960s has not been completely dampened by the economic crisis of the past dozen years.

One of the significant pieces of evidence for this has been the steady decline in male labor force participation rates. During the 1970s many of these men simply gave up on what they regarded as the rat race of permanent, full-time employment. While some popular books and articles spoke of these drop-outs as 'living without work',[14] the truth was that their relationship to work had not ended but changed. In a 1977 article entitled, 'The Great Male Cop-Out from the Work Ethic', *Business Week* magazine noted that these drop-outs from the official labor force were actually 'off-and-on workers' and observed:

> Sometimes the work is legal, such as carpentry, and sometimes . . . it is illegal, such as selling drugs. Either way, men in this group work as unofficially and occasionally self-employed persons, thus evading labor-force statistics . . . In a few areas, work-force dropouts have begun to form a substantial percentage of the population. In the Florida Keys, an entire subculture of boat dwellers has abandoned regular work for a life of sailing, fishing, and odd-jobbing.[15]

Aside from those who had significant savings and other wealth to draw on, much of this 'subculture' was dependent on government benefits as well as irregular work. The 1970s were also a time when US social spending ceased to be concentrated on the poor and predominantly non-white population.[16] This was partly an inevitable result of economic conditions, but it was also prompted by a new attitude on the part of those who had lost faith in the work ethic. Programs such as unemployment insurance, food stamps, and disability, lost much of their stigma for the so-called middle class. While some people needed those payments merely to survive, growing numbers of others sought to use them to restructure their work lives. A San Francisco musician described his way of earning a living to a magazine reporter:

I'll work a gig on the books, and when it ends I'll collect unemployment insurance. While that continues, I'll take gigs off the books, and when the unemployment money runs out, I'll do another job on the books to qualify again.[17]

This statement reflects an extraordinary change of values. A regular job is no longer one's primary activity, the basis of one's social identity. Rather it is often simply a means to qualify for unemployment compensation. While it is true that the Right has made much of such 'cheating' in its efforts to cut back on social spending, it would be naive to deny that such behavior exists among large numbers of people. Some of the same workers who might, a decade ago, have expended much energy fulminating against 'welfare cheats' are themselves now on the dole. Some may bitterly resent the fact, but others have come to embrace it as part of a new 'lifestyle'. In fact, partial dependence on government benefits is yet another characteristic of the lives of the poor that has extended to much larger portions of the population. This is not to say that class differences or inequality in the distribution of income have disappeared; it simply means that a fragmented and precarious relationship to work and income has become more common throughout advanced capitalist societies. Just as the model of the nuclear family has come to represent only a small minority of US households, so the model of the full-time, permanent 'career' job is relevant to smaller and smaller numbers of workers.

The quotation from the San Francisco musician also illustrates the way in which the underground economy has become part of the new calculus of work. Off-the-books employment is but another aspect of the varied ways in which people are earning their living. It may or may not be the case that working off the books provides greater income than doing the same thing in a regular job. What is almost certain is that the unofficial arrangement can be done under time conditions that are more to the worker's liking.

Instability and irregularity in employment, which was at the root of the marginalization of the ghetto populations of the US, is, in a different form, now a relatively desirable arrangement for many others. In some instances, the willingness to toil in such a way may be the only way for someone to qualify for a good regular job.

Many employers will take someone on as a freelancer or a temp or an occasional worker in order to test the person out before making the commitment that hiring someone permanently entails. Or else it may be that some of the most desirable work in the regular economy is only available intermittently. This is certainly the case in theatre, film and other branches of the performing arts, where at any given time the large majority of the people involved in these fields are officially unemployed. Their ability to be available when opportunities come along is often based on off-the-books work that can be left and re-entered without much difficulty.

We have come a long way from the classical Marxist labor force consisting simply of those who are regularly employed and others in various forms of the reserve army. While the dynamics of the accumulation process that Marx uncovered have not disappeared entirely, the nature of wage-labor and unemployment has undergone some fundamental changes. The combined effect of expanded precarious work in regular jobs, wider use of government benefits, hustling, and the underground economy add up to something that looks very different from the traditional labor market. To the extent that capital uses the new arrangements to increase the degree of exploitation, the new situation is simply an erosion of the power of the workers. But insofar as people are able to turn the new forms of income-generating activity to their advantage, the structure is less of a *market* and more of a terrain in the struggle for some measure of social autonomy.

3. The tax revolt and the sweatshop

On the simplest level, the underground economy is tax evasion. People are trading and working off the books because by doing so they avoid handing over a share of their income to the state. For many students of the subject this is considered an adequate explanation of the phenomenon. Everyone knows, they say, that the tax burden rose rapidly in the 1970s and people had to resort to dishonesty to maintain their standard of living. In the US the crusade known as supply-side economics made the notion of oppressive taxes its main article of faith and used it to help get Ronald Reagan elected to the White House in 1980. Reagan, in turn, suggested that his tax cuts would, among other things, bring underground business back into the sunlight.

An assessment of the causes of the underground economy, then, has to begin with consideration of the tax question. The traditional view of taxation is that it is a mechanism used by the state to obtain the resources necessary to carry out its basic functions, especially maintaining domestic order and protecting itself against foreign enemies. For most of the history of capitalist society, government revenues were gathered through indirect levies such as tariffs and excise taxes. It was as a result of popular opposition to these kinds of taxes, which were and are notoriously regressive, that progressive individual income tax schemes were established early in this century in the US and the UK.

Yet it was only after the Second World War that governments began moving toward mass taxation through payroll taxes as well as personal income taxes. At the same time, the use of tax revenues has gone far beyond the financing of the police and the army. As the functions of the state have grown more and more elaborate and integral to the economy, there has been a tendency for the public sector to appropriate a greater share of national income. Increasing dependence on the taxation of workers and the general population was an important element of the Keynesian system of political economy that served as the basis of postwar economic development. Tax revenues obtained from pay packets financed the expansion of the military and the growth of the welfare state.

The two tax rebellions

While individuals of moderate means were shouldering an increasing share of the fiscal burden, the demands on the corporate sector were becoming much lighter. During the 1970s social security payments as a portion of all taxes climbed to over 20 per cent for the OECD nations as a group. By 1980 that figure was more than 40 per cent in France, 38 per cent for the Netherlands, and 34 per cent for West Germany. At the same time, the share represented by corporate taxes fell to less than eight per cent.[1]

During the 1970s the tax burden on workers grew even worse as a result of the phenomenon known as bracket creep. In an inflationary period, rising nominal wage rates push people into higher tax brackets, and the result is a decline in one's after-tax real income. In the US this process was alleviated somewhat by changes in the tax code and eventually cuts in the basic rates. Yet even the substantial Reagan tax cuts of 1981 were barely enough to offset the combined effects of bracket creep and rising social security contributions. When increased state and local taxes were taken into account, some people were facing a heavier tax bite than before Reagan took office.[2]

The escalating fiscal demands of government gave rise in a number of countries to organized tax revolts. Yet many of these movements were instigated by the Right and were oriented more to the interests of the middle class than to those of workers; in the case of the famous Proposition 13 in California which put a ceiling on rates, the main beneficiaries were large property owners and corporations.

Many workers chose to ignore the organized rebellion and respond to the fiscal squeeze in a quiet, individual way. Experiencing the effects of accelerating living costs and rising unemployment as well as higher taxes, people engaged in a do-it-yourself tax revolt by simply working off the books.

The underground economy differs from an organized tax revolt in that it is not simply a means by which people lower their tax rates; rather it is a way of eliminating levies altogether. In many instances it is only the complete absence of taxation that makes the work worthwhile. This is most clearly the case with many moonlighters, who already have a basic income and some degree of financial security. The recourse to a second occupation off the books is primarily a matter of gaining additional cash income.

For many others, it is the undeclared character of informal work rather than the lack of taxes that is central to its appeal. People who need to remain officially unemployed or out of the labor force in order to go on collecting some government benefit require employment whose existence cannot be detected by government authorities. There are also cases in which moonlighters can only carry out that work off the books because of prohibitions against second occupations, part-time work or the performance of certain kinds of activity without a license.

Despite the fiscal incentive, it seems unlikely that large numbers of people voluntarily give up regular occupations to work off the books. A veteran wage-earner who suddenly disappears from the tax rolls is bound to come under the scrutiny of government investigators. Beyond that, the conditions of economic existence in the underground, except for people with special skills, are precarious enough for anyone who has a choice to be hesitant to depend on informal activity as his or her sole means of support.

There are some workers who may not have a choice at all; for example, immigrants without work permits. Shut out from the regular labor force and missing out on government benefits, informal work may be the only kind of gainful activity available. The employers who are making such work available are often doing so only because it is to be done off the books. If the boss has to respect labor laws and other government regulations as well as pay taxes, the chances are that the job – and perhaps the entire enterprise – would evaporate.

All this indicates that, although tax evasion is an element of informal sector activity, the existence of a rising tax burden is not a sufficient explanation of the growth of the underground economy. From the point of view of the worker, the decision to toil off the books may be as much a matter of keeping that activity secret as earning tax-free income. In terms of employers' motivations, the quest for greater flexibility in the use of labor may be stronger than the desire to reduce fiscal payments to the government.

The underground economy is a kind of tax revolt, but it is also much more than that. It is a symptom of a chronic economic crisis afflicting most of the developed countries as well as a part of the restructuring of labor markets and forms of production taking place in the course of that crisis. It is within that larger context that a fuller explanation of the rise of the underground economy can be found.

No work, new work

The past decade has witnessed the steady abandonment of the promise that the political economies of the developed countries could provide anything close to full employment. In recent years jobless rates have reached postwar records in many countries and in some instances approached the levels experienced during the Depression of the 1930s. There is an abundance of evidence that current-day capital is tending, as a result of new technology, economic stagnation and changing patterns of investment, to create larger surplus labor populations in the developed world. A generation of young people is leaving school with dim prospects of finding secure employment.

The relationship of this situation to the growth of the underground economy is clear. The scarcity of regular job possibilities forces people into unconventional and unofficial means of earning income. Whether the activity is full-time underground work or odd jobs off the books, the informal sector has absorbed countless workers expelled from the regular economy. The reliance on undocumented income has been all the greater due to the fiscal austerity that governments have imposed amid the economic crisis. Cutbacks in benefits have removed much of the cushion that redundant workers and their families enjoyed during previous recessions in the postwar period. One has had to be out of work longer, more completely devoid of resources, and more thoroughly miserable before government aid would be granted.

The rise in unemployment and the fiscal crisis have received considerable attention and thus need no further elaboration here.

Yet there is another aspect of transformation of capitalism in the 1970s and 1980s that has been the subject of much less analysis. This involves the growth, amid economies still dominated by large enterprises, of productive activities carried out by small firms operating under old-fashioned conditions. This marginal sector, previously thought to be a disappearing part of the advanced economies, has taken on a much greater role. This segment of business tends to employ people under conditions much inferior to those in large workplaces, thus giving rise to a polarization of the labor force. One writer has called the phenomenon 'neo-dualism'.[3]

Modern capitalism has always included a small business sector alongside the corporate giants that have come to dominate the economy during this century. Whether regarded as a relic of an earlier socio-economic stage or an exception to the pattern of concentration and centralization of production, small firms have not been seen as playing a major role in the accumulation process. They dominated particular industries that, for various reasons, did not become highly monopolized, and their low rates of profit forced them to rely on cheap labor. They were the main users of the lower-paid workers in the so-called secondary labor market.

Over the past 15 years this realm of marginal and precarious labor has been expanding dramatically. Many industries in the developed countries have experienced heightened competition from the third world and have responded with a furious effort to lower labor costs. As the numbers of well-paid and secure jobs in industries such as auto and steel have been steadily reduced, that augmentation of employment which has taken place has been concentrated in work that is poorly paid, unprotected and irregular. The sweatshop has made a resounding comeback in the developed countries, depriving many workers of the legal and contractual rights that the labor movement successfully fought for over many decades.

What is new about the renaissance of substandard working conditions is that big business as well as small has sought to take advantage of this cheapening of labor. Large corporations have also been buffeted by stronger foreign competition along with a high degree of worker militancy in some countries. In response, major companies have entered into a kind of conspiracy with small entrepreneurs. The 'plot' goes under the name of subcontracting.

Wherever possible, work has been relocated from large factories to small operations where the labor force is unorganized and in a weaker position to determine working conditions and pay.[4] Sometimes the smaller plant is formally owned by the larger corporation but more often the work is farmed out to a separate entity not bound by any contractual agreements unions may have with the big company. The small firm may be thoroughly dependent on the larger one for its business, yet they are legally distinct.

This decentralization of production occurred most dramatically in Italy (see chapter 7), but the same process gradually appeared in the US, Britain and other advanced countries as well. Japanese industry is one of the most enthusiastic practitioners of this system. As many as a third of the vehicles sold with Toyota and Nissan labels have at times been manufactured in large part by employees of other, smaller firms.[5] The subcontracting companies do not provide guaranteed employment, as the big firms do, and their workers are paid much less. In some cases the subcontracted labor is brought right into the factory of the large company. At Nippon Steel, permanent workers with lifetime jobs have at times worked side by side with temporary workers, the two groups distinguishable only by their different color hardhats.[6]

European and American businesses have, while embracing Eastern management techniques, adopted this dirty secret of Japanese industry as well. As the *Economist* has cheerfully reported:

> Expensive, full-time workers are being turned into cheaper, independent subcontractors by a growing number of companies in Europe. Skilled, white-collar workers can cost employers up to three times their basic salary in office space, fringe benefits and other overheads. By turfing them out and signing contracts for their services, companies can cut costs and still retain people they can trust.[7]

The system has also worked to the advantage of transnational corporations, allowing them to obtain labor in the third world at rates even lower than the rock-bottom wages paid in the factories they directly own. (More on this in chapter 8.)

For some workers, particularly white males who were previously employed in the larger workplaces, subcontracting means a deterioration of working conditions and a decline in wages; but the process does not necessarily subject them to the most oppressive of conditions. By contrast, the workers sought by some especially labor-intensive industries are placed in situations in which all the basic rights of labor established in the regular economy are ignored. For these workers, who are predominantly female, non-white and of immigrant status, the fruit of decentralization is the sweatshop.

Previously thought to be a relic of an earlier period of capitalism, small fly-by-night enterprises have proliferated in a number of industries during the past dozen years. Hidden away in old loft buildings in the poorer parts of town, the sweatshops have taken on a greater presence in cities such as Los Angeles, Paris and London. New York City alone has been estimated to contain some 3,000 sweatshops employing 50,000 workers.[8] The nightmarish working conditions of unregulated capitalism – 70-hour weeks, near starvation wages, ruthless employers – are once again the subject of press and academic reports in the developed countries. Barbro Hoel found the following conditions in her study of clothing sweatshops in Coventry:

> Not only do they [the workers, Asian women] receive poor wages for a long and strenuous week, but in many of the factories which run into financial trouble at various stages, they do not even get their full pay for the work done. One worker described how the boss's wife regularly took insufficient cash from the bank to pay everybody, so that money was taken from several paypackets to make up the missing amount, with 'promises' of the difference (perhaps half the wage) at a later date.[9]

The entrepreneurs of the marginal sector make extensive use of the large numbers of foreigners who have migrated into Europe and North America since the 1960s. While many of the early migrants were absorbed into regular enterprises (at the lowest levels), the economic crisis that started in the mid-1970s eliminated much of the work for which foreigners were once recruited. In

Europe, many thousands of 'guest workers' lost their jobs and were pressured to return to their native countries. Many refused forced repatriation and faced the prospect of earning a living without a work permit.[10] In the US, several million Mexicans and other Latin Americans, fleeing economic and political oppression, have flooded into states such as Texas and California, taking over the worst jobs in agriculture, services and light industry. Throughout the developed world, undocumented foreign workers, together with 'legal' workers at the bottom of the labor market hierarchy, have given the new sweatshop entrepreneurs an ample labor pool from which to select their victims.

Exploitation hits home

The resurrection of the sweatshop has been accompanied in recent years by the revival of another supposedly anachronistic form of production: home work. Because of its labor-intensive production process and its fragmented industrial structure, the clothing industry has taken the lead in this practice as well. Thousands, perhaps millions, of women throughout the developed countries have found that doing waged work in the home is the only way for them to earn essential income. Many of the women are housewives whose domestic responsibilities prevent them from going out to work; others are immigrant women whose patriarchal customs discourage women from working outside the home. Yet others are illegal immigrants who fear detection by the government if they work in a factory.[11]

Whatever their motivation for engaging in the activity, home workers are the most vulnerable members of the labor force. In some countries, such as the US, industrial home work is itself largely illegal. The worker thus has no recourse to government intervention over wages and working conditions. Where the practice is not against the law, such as in Britain, the home worker is caught in an ambiguous role between that of worker and that of a self-employed person. State regulation is not vigorously enforced, and trade union organization is severely limited. Whether functioning legally or illegally, the home worker is usually at the mercy of her boss, who knows she has no alternative but to accept his terms. Compelled to work on a piecework basis, the home worker often ends up with wages far inferior to that of the lowest-paid factory hands. A survey of 500 home workers by the UK Department of Employment (published in 1982) found that 73 per cent of the women were earning less than £35 a week. At the same time, research in New York found cases of home workers earning less than $2 an hour.[12]

It is difficult to estimate how many people are engaged in home labor. The illegal and therefore surreptitious status of the practice in the US makes measurement particularly elusive. National estimates are rare, but government officials have suggested a figure of 50,000 for the clothing industry of New York City alone.[13] In Britain the problems of definition and of getting women to overcome the inclination to conceal the activity have given rise to wide variations in the estimates. The latest government calculations put the figure at 251,000 in England and Wales.[14] The ranks of home workers are perhaps greatest in Italy (see chapter 7), where at least one million women are believed to earn a living that way.

In many cases home work is closely linked with sweatshops. Women who are unable to earn a decent wage in a marginal factory take additional work home with them. The entrepreneurs of the small firms may combine production on their own premises with work farmed out to women toiling at home. The impresarios of both forms of super-exploitation are often, like their employees, of immigrant status. It is a common pattern for a sweatshop or a home work operation to be set up, for instance, by a Greek-Cypriot man in London or a Korean man in New York who will make exclusive use of women workers of the same ethnic background. The quest for profit overwhelms any sense of national solidarity.[15]

Home work goes high-tech

The resurgence of industrial home labor is not limited to those sectors of the economy that have traditionally made some use of the practice. It has also appeared in the US amid the high-tech world of electronics.

The US semiconductor industry grew up in the area south of San Francisco now immortalized as Silicon Valley. The popular image engendered of this area was one where small, brash entrepreneurial companies sprang up overnight, and on the basis of a new chip or disk young engineers became multimillionaires. While such success stories are not entirely imaginary, the reality of Silicon Valley has not been so rosy. First of all, the devices designed by the brilliant and now rich young engineers have to be produced in quantity by someone if the company is to prosper. While it is true that much of the assembly work has been transferred to low-wage havens in South East Asia, there are also assembly lines in Silicon Valley. The workers staffing those operations are not the ones driving around in Jaguars. They are often recent immigrants, including Filipinos and Vietnamese refugees, who are paid close to the minimum wage and are without union protection. The work itself often turns out to be quite dangerous, because of the toxic and carcinogenic substances used in semiconductor fabrication.[16]

In keeping with the trend toward decentralization, parts of this production have begun to be transferred to workers toiling in their homes. According to an article in the *Los Angeles Times*:

> Home workers constitute a growing underground market of cheap labor in America's most glamorous high-technology business. It is a black market based on direct cash payments to workers, often recent immigrants or undocumented aliens.[17]

Semiconductor manufacturers have learned that certain labor-intensive aspects of their production process, such as 'stuffing' (attaching integrated circuits to printed circuit boards), can be profitably farmed out to home workers. The local newspaper, the *San Jose Mercury News*, which did an exposé of these practices in 1980, reported that 'knowledgeable industry sources estimate that thousands of people and millions of dollars are involved'.[18] Home workers, who are invariably paid off the books, are, like their factory counterparts, often exposed to hazardous substances such as fumes from soldering or toxic solvents that have to be kept warm on the kitchen stove.[19]

The development of new computer technology has also made it possible for business to relocate clerical work in the home. Already, several thousand women in the US and the UK earn a wage by processing data on terminals that are electronically linked to a company's offices. These typists, claims processors, data entry clerks and other 'information workers' are usually denied sick leave, paid vacations and most other fringe benefits. They often pay a rental charge to their employer for the use of his terminal. Frequent articles in management literature have been touting home work as a way of cutting costs and getting around the problems of absenteeism and tardiness.

If for the boss electronic home work means higher profits, for the worker the arrangement means isolation and an end to the socializing and informal co-operation that are often the only things that make a job bearable. In an advertisement for Lanier Business Products' Telestaff System, the supplier of home work equipment praised the virtues of a physically dispersed labor force: 'The Telestaff Station. It brings work to your office. Not people.'[20]

It is true that some women who need to earn a wage would prefer not having to report to an office. This form of employment may be the only type available for mothers of young children with no access to day care. Working at home also allows one to avoid rigid job schedules, the daily journey to work, and the need to get dressed up to go to the office. The most enthusiastic proponents of home work, such as the futurologist Alvin Toffler, see it as an important step toward the re-creation of a home-centred society.[21] Yet the prospect of remaining at home may not be so appealing to a generation of women who have been abandoning full-time housework in record numbers and rushing into the paid labor market. The rise of electronic (and traditional) home work can have the effect of pushing women into dead-end jobs and depriving them of the measure of social power that working with others provides. Toffler's 'electronic cottage' could turn out to be nothing more than a personal electronic sweatshop.

Subcontracting, sweatshops, home work. They all add up to a very different model of accumulation from the old notion of a relentless drive towards centralization of production within a system of protected labor. Motivated by a burning need to gain greater flexibility and substantially lower costs in the use of labor, many sectors of business have remolded themselves in ways that counteract the previous tendencies of the system. Large companies and their smaller counterparts have joined one another to undermine the power of workers in the name of enhancing competitiveness. Little thought has been given to the impact of these changes on the people subjected to them in the workplace. The labor movement has been set back decades as workers have found themselves toiling in conditions reminiscent of the nineteenth century.

The underground economy is part and parcel of this transformation. While not all firms engaging in subcontracting and decentralized production do so off the books, there has been a rapid growth in the number of enterprises seeking to carry out their business totally free of state inspection. Operating underground allows the new marginal businesses to circumvent both traditional worker protections such as minimum wage levels and the new forms of labor legislation – covering areas such as occupational health and racial and sexual discrimination – that were enacted in many countries in the 1970s.

By restructuring production, business puts the worker at a disadvantage; by doing so and also going off the books, small entrepreneurs render the labor force much weaker. People doing sweatshop labor or home work for a marginal firm are in a poor position to fight for better conditions since any attempt to assert collective rights could prompt the entrepreneur to pick up stakes and open shop somewhere else.

The informal economy is not identical to the process of restructuring. Some decentralized operations remain on the books, and some underground practices take place outside the context of marginal production. Yet the two are closely related. Operating a business off the books – i.e. without any state regulation or union involvement – is the logical conclusion of the restructuring process. It represents the ultimate goal of the profit-maximizing entrepreneur: proverbial *free* enterprise.

The type of restructuring that has taken place makes it possible for firms that cannot or do not want to go underground to take advantage of unprotected labor nonetheless. Subcontracting permits larger companies to keep their hands clean and let smaller, shady firms do the dirty work of running sweatshops and home work operations. The increasing dependence of regular enterprises on marginal and underground labor suggests that the dividing line between the formal and informal sectors is far from clear.

The underground economy, then, is part of a larger transformation of contemporary capitalism. Although it often takes the form of tax evasion, what is going on is much more significant than people fiddling the revenue authorities. A profound power shift in class relations is taking place, and the informal economy is contributing mightily to it.

4. Measuring the unmeasurable

Modern social science has become wedded to quantitative methods. Thanks to computers and the refinement of statistical techniques, sociologists and political scientists and economists are as preoccupied as physicists with measuring the things they study. The truths of these disciplines are more and more evaluated in terms of probabilities, correlations and standard deviations. Conclusions without numbers attached to them are viewed with suspicion.

The obsession with size carries over into examination of phenomena that, by their nature, defy accurate measurement. Academics build careers on attempts to improve estimates of criminal activities or illegal immigration. They often serve on government bodies charged with making 'educated guesses' about the extent of clandestine behavior – conclusions which are subsequently cited as authoritative, no matter how dubious were the assumptions on which they were based.

This scenario has been played out most recently with regard to the underground economy. Not much thought was given to the phenomenon until large numbers were attributed to it. In the US the process started in early 1978, after economist Peter Gutmann did some quick calculations and presented the startling conclusion that nearly $200 billion in unreported income – about 10 per cent of the official gross national product (GNP) – was being hidden from the Internal Revenue Service. A year later the measurement game was initiated in Britain by Sir William Pile, chairman of the Inland Revenue, who told parliament that it 'was not implausible' that the informal economy was equal to 7½ per cent of gross domestic product (GDP).

In the following years, the considerable attention paid to the underground economy in both countries has almost exclusively dealt with the question of size. Economists and government officials have engaged in sometimes heated debate about the numbers, while little work has been done on explaining how the informal economy functions and what effects it has on the society at large.

This chapter will summarize and assess the quantitative methods that have been proposed. While not dismissing the measurement effort, the concern here is to urge some caution in the numbers game. There is also a need to be much clearer about what exactly one is attempting to measure. As a relatively new and somewhat elusive phenomenon, the underground economy has been discussed with terminology sorely lacking in consistency and clarity. Before looking at the quantitative approaches it would be useful to sort out the concepts relating to the measurement process.

Underground national accounting

There are two major ways in which the underground economy may be viewed. On the one hand, it is *national income* overlooked by those who perform the official calculations of a country's total economic activity. In this sense it represents a shortcoming in conventional measurement techniques and may be defined as an *understatement of true GNP or GDP*. (For the purposes of this book the two need not be distinguished. GNP will be generally used, while specific references to the UK will follow the custom of using GDP.)

On the other hand, the phenomenon may be put in terms of income that is not reported to revenue authorities for tax purposes. The underground economy thus represents a *shortcoming in tax compliance* and may be defined as the amount of *unreported income*.

From a quantitative point of view, national income and taxable income overlap to a great extent but are far from identical. There are elements of GNP which are not taxable and forms of taxable income which are excluded from the national accounts. Discussion of the size of the underground economy ought not to use the two concepts interchangeably.

With regard to the GNP approach, it is not sufficient simply to distinguish between what is measured and what is not. For years the government bodies responsible for the national accounts – the Bureau of Economic Analysis (part of the Commerce Department) in the US and the Central Statistical Office in the UK – have recognized the existence of unreported income and have quietly made relatively slight adjustments to the GNP figures to reflect their estimate of its extent.

There may be some argument whether this additional income is truly measured or simply guessed at, but the fact remains that official GNP numbers already include conservative estimates of the size of the underground economy.

With regard to the unreported income approach, there has been a tendency by some economists and government officials to estimate how much public treasuries are losing as a result of underground activities. The Inland Revenue estimated in 1980 that the informal economy was costing the British government £3,500 million a year in lost revenues. American commentators are fond of claiming that if taxes were paid on all underground activity, the federal budget deficit could be wiped out.

On a purely theoretical level this is a valid enough exercise, assuming one has taken into account that portion of unreported income that would not be subject to tax even if it were declared. Yet, in a practical sense, it is a mistake to assume that concealed income could, to any great degree, be recaptured and subjected to taxation. Much underground activity takes place precisely because it is free from taxation; otherwise it would cease to exist.

Measurement gambits

With this groundwork set out it is possible to review more critically the various techniques that have been proposed for measuring the underground economy. These methods fall into three major categories, with a number of variations:

- indirect approaches which look at traces of underground activity in economic aggregates such as the money supply;
- indirect approaches based on discrepancies between expenditure and income;
- direct approaches based on the amounts of hidden income discovered in intensive official investigation of small samples of taxpayers.

Several other measurement issues – labor force figures and estimates of illegal activities – are dealt with in other chapters.

Currency in circulation

The roots of the research on the underground economy can be found in the discovery by the US economists in the late 1960s of a peculiar fact. Despite the rapid spread of checking accounts, credit cards and automatic funds transfer, the amount of currency in circulation remained unusually high. Articles in various Federal Reserve bank publications puzzled over why people kept, on average, $237 (in 1968) in cash in their possession – cash that earned no interest and might be lost or stolen. Cash in circulation per capita had been steadily rising since 1961 after remaining fairly constant since the end of the Second World War.

The analysts of the early 1970s considered a wide range of explanations as to why people were keeping so much money outside their bank accounts. They debated how much of it represented a store of value (i.e. hoarding) and how much was needed as a means of exchange. They tried to link the rise to higher income and price levels, the degree of urbanization, foreign holdings of dollars – even the spread of coin-operated vending machines. But none of these factors was adequate to explain the magnitude of the rise.

Only hesitantly did the economists acknowledge that unreported income and tax evasion might be part of the equation. They did readily admit that the previous occasion when currency in circulation took a big leap was during the Second World War. The rationing of commodities during the early 1940s gave rise to an extensive black market on the homefront which required large amounts of cash to operate.

That such a breakdown in the social order had emerged once again was next to impossible for mainstream economists to imagine. A 1972 article on the currency mystery in a newsletter of Morgan Guaranty bank concluded nervously:

> Conceding that a certain amount of cash is desired to cover
> up illicit operations or to cheat the tax collector, the sharp
> rise in cash, big bills and all, can hardly be explained by such

thievery unless one assumes that people somehow have gone bad on a mammoth scale. Happily, such a bleak assessment lacks any corroboration.[1]

Other observers, less confident of the morality of the majority of Americans, continued to look at the 'sinister' implications of the ever-growing volume of cash in circulation. They focused on the fact that within the expanding pool of cash the steepest increase was for large denomination notes – $50 and $100. From 1960 to 1970 the stock of smaller denomination notes ($1 to $10) rose 37 per cent, while big bills increased more than 75 per cent.[2] By 1976 there were about 210 million $100 bills and 160 million $50 bills in the hands of the population.

The emphasis on the big bill phenomenon appeared most clearly in the work of economist James Henry. Writing in 1976, he argued that the increasing demand for $50 and $100 notes could only be explained by an expansion of profit-oriented crime and tax evasion – activities which required the use of cash in order to avoid leaving traceable records.[3] (Especially in the case of outright criminal transactions, such as heroin dealing, sellers are not likely to trust their buyers to the point of accepting checks.)

Using an equation that tied the demand for large denomination notes to 'legitimate' factors such as price levels, personal consumption expenditures and federal income tax revenues, Henry calculated the extra demand for big bills that resulted from tax evasion. Deriving a range of estimates for unreported income in 1973 from about $16 billion to $70 billion, he proposed that 'a reasonable figure for the amount of tax evasion using bills of $50 and higher might be $30 billion a year.'

Turning then to organized crime as the other major component of the illegitimate demand for big bills, Henry used a hodgepodge of evidence to back the assertion that profit-motivated crime amounted to another $30 billion a year.

Henry's writing was primarily concerned with using the analysis as a basis for urging the federal government to carry out a recall of large bills, an act which he claimed would undermine the anti-social behavior of tax evaders and the mafia by making their illegitimately-accumulated cash worthless. He played down the extent to which smaller-time operators, such as moonlighting skilled workers, might be contributing to the additional demand for cash. He also did not emphasize the fact that his estimate of $60 billion in unreported income suggested the existence of a realm of economic activity equal to nearly five per cent of the official GNP. The term underground economy had not yet come into use, and Henry's work attracted little attention.

The currency ratio

The event responsible for generating wide public interest in the growth of off-the-books activity in the US was the publication at the end of 1977 of a three-page article by economist Peter Gutmann.[4] He confidently asserted a specific and large figure for the size of what he chose to call the subterranean economy – $176 billion in 1976. The claim ended up receiving an extraordinary amount of publicity in the press and the broadcast media, apparently based on nearly universal acceptance of the notion that unreported income had suddenly reached extraordinary levels in the US. It was as if observers of the social and economic scene had known for a long time that some important changes were taking place – changes they could not quite articulate – and it took a catalyst such as Gutmann's short article to clear the clouds.

Where Gutmann's argument turned out to be more controversial was in the exact way he presumed to estimate the size of the subterranean economy. He started out by returning to the growth of cash in circulation. Yet for him there was no mystery. In the very first paragraph of his piece he stated flatly: 'This currency lubricates a vast amount of non-reported income and non-reported work and employment.'

Like Henry, Gutmann assumed the only way to measure underground activity was indirectly, by looking at the additional demand for currency created by those who had to carry out their illegitimate transactions in cash. But instead of looking at the absolute amount of cash in circulation, Gutmann chose to examine the composition of the money supply, i.e. the ratio of cash to funds in checking accounts (otherwise known as current accounts or demand deposits).

Assuming that there was no underground economy in the US in the years immediately preceding the Second World War (since income tax rates were still very low), Gutmann took the ratio during that period as normal. Noting then that the ratio had risen substantially by the middle of the 1970s, Gutmann asserted that in 1976 there was about $29 billion (of all denominations) in circulation beyond what was required for legitimate transactions. And, taking for granted that subterranean cash circulated at the same rate as the 'legitimate money stock', Gutmann was able to conclude that the subterranean GNP was equal to more than 10 per cent of officially calculated national income.

There was grace in the simplicity of Gutmann's method, yet upon closer examination it turned out to have a number of major flaws. There are several reasons for the decline in the currency ratio that have nothing to do with a subterranean economy, and it is suspicious that related ratios such as currency to GNP show no consistent pattern of increase. Gutmann also failed to take into account unreported income that was already estimated in the national accounts.[5]

Despite the shortcomings of his specific methodology, Gutmann does deserve credit for stimulating a variety of other indirect measurement efforts and for focusing public attention on the phenomenon of unreported income. Some of the economists who entered the field made careful refinements to the currency equation,[6] while others made bold forays into macroeconomic speculation. The most notorious of the latter group was Edgar Feige, who had set out in 1978 to rebut Gutmann's arguments for the existence of a large underground economy. Once he delved into the subject, however, Feige became a convert.[7]

Basing his analysis on an estimate of total transactions in the economy, and taking into account such factors as the physical composition of paper money, Feige went even further than Gutmann. His calculation of an underground economy of more than $700 billion in 1978 – nearly 27 per cent of official GNP – stands as the highest estimate made by a respectable economist in the US. Feige's method was subjected to as much criticism as Gutmann's, but he remained undaunted. A few years later he applied his technique to the UK, and the resulting estimate of 15 per cent of GDP set off a furore in parliament and the press.

Feige's analysis, like that of Henry, Gutmann and others, was based on some questionable assumptions about the rate of circulation of money. Economists have a hard enough time estimating what they call the velocity of currency for entirely above-ground transactions, so it is no surprise that the use of this concept for measuring concealed activities should be so controversial. The inability to know how frequently money changes hands is a major flaw in the indirect measurement process and is part of the reason why the results of these quantitative gambits remain inconclusive.

Discrepancies between expenditure and income

In Britain, the indirect methods of measuring unreported activity have taken a different tack. Here, analysis assumes that while people may be tempted to conceal income, they are less likely to hide their true expenditure levels when interviewed in the government's household surveys. The Central Statistical Office (CSO) uses the discrepancy between the aggregate amount of reported income and the invariably higher amount of reported expenditures to make adjustments to preliminary GDP calculations. In this way an approximation of underground activity is included in the official national accounts.

The CSO did not publicize this process until the controversy about the size of the underground economy erupted in the late 1970s. In 1980 Kerrick Macafee of the CSO published a study in which he revealed that the 1978 GDP numbers included adjustments totalling £3,640 million, the largest part of which was £2,760 million for unreported self-employment income.[8] He also noted that the CSO recognized that an additional amount of hidden activity took place through concealed expenditure (such as for illegal drugs) and concealed income in kind (fiddling). While the former is excluded by definition from GDP, the CSO did make a small further adjustment to account for the latter. Macafee declined to give an estimate of the size of the underground economy consisting of what is entered in the national accounts and what escapes entirely.

A bolder use of the income/expenditure discrepancy has been made by Andrew Dilnot and C.N. Morris of the Institute for Fiscal Studies.[9] They began on the micro rather than macro level, conducting a detailed examination of the spending patterns of 1,000 of the 7,200 households in the government's 1977 Family Expenditure Survey. The households were found to have discrepancies averaging about £30 per week between their reported income and their expenditures, after legitimate factors were taken into account (e.g. pensioners using savings for current expenses). On this basis Dilnot and Morris claimed the underground economy for the population as a whole amounted to only about £3,000 or £4,000 million, no more than three per cent of 1977 GDP.

The authors expressed confidence in their low estimates, despite the fact that participation in the Family Expenditure Survey is voluntary, and only 70 per cent of those asked agreed to cooperate. Presumably, those people with a lot to hide would tend to refuse, meaning that the results for the participants would tend to understate the true degree of unreported income.

The discrepancy measures of unreported income are a bit more convincing than currency-based techniques, given that they are linked to something solid (expenditure figures). But it is difficult to accept the assumption that people will be scrupulous in admitting their true level of expenditures to government interviewers. Many people are bound to suspect that declaring purchases significantly out of line with one's official income could lead to legal difficulty in the future. The small adjustments to GDP made by the CSO to account for concealed expenditure and concealed income in kind do not begin to approximate what is undoubtedly being hidden.[10]

Tax audits combined with expenditure surveys

Among the attempts to measure the extent of unreported income, the most ambitious has been that of the US Internal Revenue Service. The IRS is almost alone among revenue agencies of the world in the authority it has to conduct intensive audits of a sample of taxpayers (about 50,000) chosen at random. Since 1963 the agency has relied on this Taxpayer Compliance Measurement Program (TCMP) to extend the detection of unreported income (as well as exaggerated deductions) beyond what is routinely discovered through quick checks of all returns and auditing of ones with suspicious claims.[11] Tax returns chosen for the TCMP are matched against information reports that are supposed to be filed by businesses and individuals when substantial payments are made for services, dividends, interest, royalties and so forth. Because of the huge volume of such reports, the IRS has not been able to check that all of these non-wage forms of income are being declared by recipients on their tax returns; such an investigation is done rigorously for those returns examined in the TCMP.

When Gutmann, Feige and others started talking about huge amounts of unreported and untaxed income, it was TCMP data that the IRS mainly relied upon to devise its own estimate of tax evasion. (It also came to light that the Bureau of Economic Analysis was using TCMP data to make adjustments to the national accounts to account for unreported income.) In a special study issued in 1979 amid the underground economy controversy (and revised in 1983), the IRS combined TCMP data with estimates of unreported income received by the five million people believed to file no return at all.[12] The results were as follows:

Unreported legal-source income of individual filers and non-filers, 1973–81 (in millions of dollars)

	1973	1976	1979	1981
Wages and salaries	33,304	46,274	71,076	94,581
Dividends	1,920	3,638	5,528	8,747
Interest	4,440	6,763	11,548	20,479
Capital gains	5,015	9,935	16,283	17,727
Non-farm proprietor income and partnership and small business corporate income	23,906	32,565	47,246	58,400
Farm proprietor income	5,742	4,542	7,832	9,547
Informal supplier income	10,346	12,721	16,995	17,080
Pensions and annuities	3,123	4,067	6,258	8,799
Rents	1,335	2,390	2,711	3,049
Royalties	312	1,088	1,672	2,770
Estate and trust income	487	695	1,140	1,330
State income tax refunds, alimony and other income	3,990	6,857	6,260	7,166
Total Income	**93,919**	**131,535**	**194,548**	**249,675**

The amounts are substantial but they represent widely varying proportions of the total taxable income estimated for each category. To reflect this the IRS compiled what it called voluntary reporting percentages; in other words, the percentage of total taxable income which was declared, as opposed to the additional amounts detected by the IRS through TCMP investigations.

Voluntary reporting percentages for individual filers and non-filers, by source of income, 1973–81

	1973	1976	1979	1981
Wages and salaries*	95.3	94.9	94.4	93.9
Dividends	90.7	87.1	85.7	83.7
Interest	87.6	88.1	86.3	86.3
Capital gains	75.7	64.3	63.4	59.4
Non-farm proprietor income and partnership and small business corporate income	84.0	82.2	80.7	78.7
Farm proprietor income	88.6	92.6	89.5	88.3
Informal supplier income	20.7	20.7	20.7	20.7
Pensions and annuities*	83.5	86.9	86.7	86.9
Rents	94.7	94.0	95.4	95.6
Royalties	74.3	65.6	64.2	61.2
Estate and trust income	82.0	79.2	75.7	76.2
State income tax refunds, alimony and other income	66.0	55.2	62.3	62.0
Total Income	**91.2**	**90.4**	**89.8**	**89.3**

* After adjustments for pension income misreported as wage income.

These numbers show that, while the absolute amounts of unreported income detected by the IRS in many categories were quite high, these did not always correspond to large percentages of the total income of those sorts. Yet even in the categories subject to withholding (PAYE), especially wages and salaries, people are trying to conceal a steadily increasing percentage of that income.

The IRS research team acknowledged that a tool other than the

TCMP and the Exact Match File (the technique used for non-filers) was needed for estimating the unreported income of an important group in the underground economy, namely small-scale entrepreneurs who did not operate as regular firms and thus escaped all government information gathering efforts. These are the informal suppliers listed in the tables above. To get at their activities the IRS turned from income to expenditure. It commissioned a study from the University of Michigan in which, after training in detecting when suppliers were likely to be operating off the books, several thousand households were surveyed on their spending patterns. The results of that survey, extended to the population as a whole, were as follows:

Value of household purchases from informal vendors by types of goods and services, 1981 (in millions of dollars)

Home repair and addition	12,245
Food	9,003
Child care	4,995
Domestic service	3,882
Auto repair	2,810
Sidewalk vendor goods	1,782
Flea market goods	1,698
Lawn maintenance	1,447
Lessons	933
Fuel	749
Appliance repair	744
Adult care	442
Cosmetic service	411
Sewing and related	392
Catering	300
Total	**41,793**

After adjusting for an assumed level of business expenses for the informal suppliers and subtracting the portions voluntarily reported and received by non-filers (the latter being already counted), the IRS derived an estimate of about $14 billion in taxable income received by these small-scale operations.[13]

Of all the techniques surveyed, the IRS approach is the most impressive. The TCMP component, in particular, inspires confidence because it is rooted in something real – documented discovery of unreported income. As long as one is willing to accept the statistical inference involved in projecting the results of 50,000 investigations to the population at large – which is, after all, the general way all economic statistics are derived – some genuine measurement seems to be going on. By contrast, calculations such as those of Gutmann and Feige seem pulled out of thin air. The IRS figures also have the advantage of being calculated strictly in terms of *taxable* income. A careful distinction is also made between unreported income flowing from legal and illegal activities. The indirect techniques allow no such specificity.

The problem with the IRS method, however, is that it is most appropriate to under-reporting of income from activities that are originally on the books, but which people try to exclude from their tax returns. It is best able to track down income for which documentation exists somewhere. The success of the measurement lies in the ability of the auditor to find that proof, which in turn depends on the resources at the disposal of the IRS staff. This measurement technique thus has the peculiarity that its efficacy is a function of IRS budgetary decisions.

When no 'paper trail' exists, this approach weakens. Regardless of how much in the way of resources is devoted to TCMP, income which is entirely off the books – unreported by both the payer and the recipient – will evade detection.

The IRS has recognized this and made a serious effort to estimate income of this sort through the improved expenditure survey. Yet once it is in this arena, which is beyond its direct investigatory scope, the IRS has less of an advantage over other explorers of the underground economy. The expenditure survey was done carefully but required some bold assumptions. Most difficult to accept is the idea that respondents were able, even with preparation, to detect when suppliers of goods and services were operating off the books and when they were not. Nevertheless, the IRS estimates are probably the best macro measures that can be made of the underground economy, short of the possibility of an effective census of that informal realm.

Because the IRS, especially in the 1983 report, limited itself to estimating taxable income, the agency did not compare its figures to the overall official GNP. Even if there are technical problems with making the comparison, it is worth noting that the estimate of $250 billion in unreported income for 1981 was equal to more than eight per cent of the official GNP. However, as mentioned earlier, the official national accounts are already adjusted (by amounts that are not published by the government) to account for unreported income detected by the TCMP. The last TCMP for which data were available to the IRS was that of 1976, when about $20 billion in unreported income was found. Projected to 1981 this figure was put by the IRS at about $37 billion.[14]

In other words, $37 billion of the estimated $250 billion in unreported income was presumably already figured into the national accounts. In percentage terms we could say that while the underground economy, by these estimates, may have equaled about 8½ per cent of stated GNP, those GNP numbers were understated by less than seven per cent (reflecting unreported income not captured by TCMP).

The ten per cent solution

Allow a few percentage points for underestimation of informal supplier income and it turns out, ironically, that the IRS direct measurement technique corroborates Gutmann's original approximation. An underground economy of this magnitude is also in keeping with impressionistic evidence. Off-the-books labor, under-reporting of income and other such practices are common, but at least in the US and Britain they are not omnipresent. The IBMs and General Electrics of the world are not teetering on the edge of extinction, nor has the state totally lost its ability to regulate and to tax.

Ten per cent is a reasonable working estimate. It does not stretch credibility but is large enough to make the underground economy a phenomenon of considerable importance. It is also consistent with the conclusion reached in the Appendix regarding the size of the informal labor force. Yet the significance of the underground sector is not only in its size. Informal activity is a key element in a broader process of restructuring that is affecting the economy as a whole.

5. The underground and the underworld

The rise of the underground economy in the late 1970s came at a time when government officials and social scientists were already sounding alarms about a rapid spread of lawlessness in many countries. Leading criminologists Sir Leon Radzinowicz and Joan King put it bluntly: 'The one thing that hits you in the eye when you look at crime on the world scale is a pervasive and persistent increase everywhere. Such exceptions as there are stand out in splendid isolation, and may soon be swamped in the rising tide.'[1] Scaremongering commentators warned of an erosion of western civilization and used the crime wave to justify repressive government policies.

While the greatest public passions were aroused about violent crimes against individuals, the business world was especially agitated about the emergence of new types of assault on property, usually lumped together under the rubric of white-collar crime. Led by the US Chamber of Commerce, American corporate representatives claimed that fraud, embezzlement, employee theft and other 'crimes against business' had reached epidemic proportions, with the mythical number of $40 billion a year presented as the cost of the phenomenon.[2]

The other kind of economic crime that flourished during the 1970s and attracted substantial official concern was the drug trade. Experts claimed that a business worth many billions of dollars a year was being conducted by outlaw entrepreneurs ranging from the mafia to individuals who grew marijuana in their back yard and peddled it to friends.

The underground economy can be seen either as a part of this expanding world of profit-oriented crime or as a related but separate phenomenon. Informal work shares with these other activities the characteristic of being illegal. In this way it is part of a more general tendency for increasing portions of the population to earn their living (or supplement legitimate income) in ways that are against the law. It would seem to be a mistake, however, to simply lump off-the-books activity together with all these other practices into one large criminal economy.

The main reason for trying to retain the distinction is that activities which are off the books are not in themselves different from legitimate economic transactions. The 'crime' usually occurs after the fact, in the failure to report the income for tax purposes. Even the lack of adherence to government regulations is not unique to the underground; above-ground entrepreneurs do the same thing whenever they can get away with it.

The refusal to make some separation between the underground economy and crime makes it impossible to see the former in relationship to the current crisis of the economy as a whole. There is nothing new about crime; illegal profit-making activities have taken place as long as there have been laws. It may be that certain kinds of outright criminal activities have risen in response to difficult economic conditions, but that is a separate issue. The informal economy is important as a transformation of *mainstream* activities of modern capitalist society rather than as an expansion of the underworld, which, however large, remains marginal.

The cash flow of crime

Having said all this, it is admittedly quite difficult to know exactly where to draw the line between the underground and the underworld. Part of the problem is that both use money and evade taxes. This fact has led some analysts of the underground economy to ignore the differences and include profit-oriented crime in their assessments of how much income is unreported. Such an approach is unavoidable in the indirect measurement techniques based on the amount of cash in circulation; money flowing out of informal work is indistinguishable from money flowing out of heroin dealing. In analyses that build on empirical evidence rather than deducing from macro data, it is possible to distinguish among types of illicit activities.

Even before the discovery of the underground economy, government officials and academics, especially in the US, expended a lot of energy trying to put a dollar figure on the volume of profit-oriented crimes such as drug dealing, illegal gambling, and prostitution. This branch of the numbers game was stimulated by the 1967 report of the President's Commission on Law Enforcement. While warning that these numbers were, at best, 'rough orders of magnitude', the Commission suggested that annual profits from illegal gambling in the US were as much as $7 billion, along with $350 million for drugs, $225 million for prostitution, and $150 million for illegally produced alcohol. It is interesting that the Commission confessed it was unable to estimate tax evasion and unreported income from legal sources.[3]

Perhaps because of the impressive-sounding name of the Commission, these figures have often been cited as authoritative or used as the basis (with an inflation factor added) for later estimates of the same phenomena. The Internal Revenue Service, however, did make use of original research undertaken during the 1970s, particularly on the drug trade. In its 1983 report the agency provided estimates on unreported income derived from three kinds of criminal pursuit (figures are in billions of dollars):[4]

	1973	1976	1979	1981
Illegal drugs	5.1	7.4	16.5	23.4
Illegal gambling	1.6	2.2	3.0	3.4
Prostitution (female only)	2.6	3.8	6.2	7.4
Total	**9.3**	**13.4**	**25.7**	**34.2**

Yet even when one has left the guessing-game realm of the President's Commission, there is still a fair amount of speculation that goes into even the most scientific-looking analyses. The techniques used by the IRS and other analysts are open to challenge on any number of technical grounds. Estimates are also subject to political pressures. In a 1979 hearing on the drug trade, the IRS commissioner was assailed by members of a Senate committee who were disappointed at what they considered the excessively low estimate made of illegal narcotics income in the original IRS study of unreported income. The committee chairman preferred to use different government estimates that were based largely on numbers from the Drug Enforcement Administration, in whose bureaucratic interest it was to have the problem seem as large as possible. The higher estimates, ranging from $44 billion to $63 billion in drug income in 1979, were seen by the senators as being more in line with the urgency they were trying to convey by holding the hearings in the first place.[5]

Even if the attempts to measure the volume of profit-oriented crime have been less than conclusive, the research on the drug trade lent some credence to the idea that unreported illegal income could be detected by looking at data on currency in circulation. In those same 1979 hearings on illegal narcotics profits, an official of the Treasury Department reported on a study that had been done of transactions at Federal Reserve offices across the country. It was found that Florida alone had consistently received more currency in deposits than the Federal Reserve had placed in circulation. That surplus had grown from $921 million in 1974 to $3.3 billion in 1978. The official stated:

> Although a variety of factors have contributed to this surplus,
> it is clear that a substantial amount is related to the
> trafficking of marijuana, cocaine and other drugs in Florida.
> Information received from Customs, DEA and other
> government sources indicates that there has been a
> tremendous influx of drug money in Florida.[6]

Picking up the thread of the big-bill theory of unreported income, the Treasury study also noted that there had been an especially rapid growth in the number of $100 bills in circulation in Florida.

Dirty money

The flow of drug money through Florida banks illustrates an important similarity between the underground economy and strictly criminal pursuits. The generation of large amounts of cash income by illicit means – whether the sale of dope, the skimming of profits from legitimate business, or doing lucrative work off the books – is pointless unless that money can be spent or invested safely. Modest amounts of money can easily be used for everyday transactions or even deposited in the bank. But beyond a certain point, a tax evader runs the risk that the discrepancy between his official income and his level of consumption will come to the attention of government investigators. The problem is greatly compounded for the drug trade, which is reputed to have a rate of return much higher than that of any legal industry. It can only reinvest so much of its enormous profits back in the business.

The need to establish some legitimacy for 'dirty money' generated by illicit transactions has given rise to a practice known as cash laundering. In the US banks are theoretically deterred from engaging in this process by federal law. The Bank Secrecy Act of 1969, for instance, requires financial institutions to file currency transaction reports whenever a customer engages in a domestic cash transaction of $10,000 or more or an international transaction of $5,000 or more. However, as the data from Florida suggest, the law is regularly being subverted. Some corrupt bankers take bribes to 'forget' to file the transaction reports or not to take notice when a customer is frequently making deposits of $9,999. Or else drug entrepreneurs allow the transaction reports to be filed and find ways of concealing their true activities from federal investigators.[7]

As loose as bank regulation is in Florida, many drug dealers and other large-scale recipients of unreported income choose the safer method of laundering their cash through foreign financial institutions in countries where the secrecy of bank transactions is adhered to. The process of transporting the currency out of the US is in effect a form of smuggling, the mirror image of one of the processes by which the funds were generated in the first place, i.e. the smuggling of illegal drugs into the country.

The Swiss bank account is the classic depository for 'dirty money', but in recent years, and especially after the Swiss amended their laws to allow disclosure of account information when organized crime may be involved, the preferred depositories have been the new tax-haven banks in places such as the Caribbean. Based in the Bahamas, the Cayman Islands, the Netherland Antilles, St. Kitts and other islands, many of these banks have been established in recent years precisely for the purpose of cash laundering. In order to thwart investigators, these banks help to establish complicated networks of dummy corporations, through which the funds are channeled numerous times until they can be returned to the US or Europe in 'clean' form. A study by the US Senate's Committee on Governmental Affairs called the use of these offshore banks the 'foreign commerce' sector of the underground economy.[8]

The attempts to measure the volume of this activity have made use of methods as arbitrary as those employed in the estimation of other clandestine practices. A figure of $50 billion a year gained some authority when it was mentioned (though labeled unreliable) in a study submitted to the Ford Foundation.[9] The Senate study just mentioned resorted to deducing the size of offshore flows from one estimate of the underground economy that included criminal as well as simply off-the-books activities. The study assumed that the foreign commerce portion of the underground was equal to the proportion that foreign trade represented for the regular economy, and in this manner derived an upper-limit figure of $43 billion for 1982.[10]

Given the costs, risks and amounts of money involved, it is likely that this more sophisticated sort of cash laundering is being carried out by organized crime rather than individual participants in criminal or underground activities. Once the mafia's funds are returned home, a great deal of money ends up invested in legal businesses. The infiltration of criminal profits into legitimate enterprise has been a matter of intense political concern in the US as far back as the 1950s, when Senator Estes Kefauver held a series of dramatic congressional hearings on the matter. Although the infiltration is often exaggerated, the range of businesses in which mafia money is known to play a role is extensive. Some of the classic examples include meat-packing, juke boxes and vending machines, mozzarella cheese (for pizza), and unions such as the Teamsters.[11]

Although these businesses are not criminal, the mafia-associated managers who run them are not exactly scrupulous in their adherence to the tax laws. This is seen perhaps most clearly in some of the casinos of Las Vegas, where organized crime, cash laundering, cash skimming, and corrupt labor unions are all mixed up together. Mafia leaders have been accused of using criminal profits to buy shares of casinos and then laundering additional funds through the gaming tables. Organized crime figures have also been charged with using Teamster pension funds to make further investments in the Las Vegas gambling business.

All of this is further evidence of the difficulty in determining the dividing line between the underground and the criminal economies. People who start off simply working off the books may stray into activities that are more serious violations of the law; criminals engaged in profit-making activities routinely evade taxes in the course of breaking other laws and then sometimes use their illicit gains to invest in legitimate businesses which may in turn accumulate unreported income.

The picture is complicated even further by the existence of other technically illegal activities that go beyond working off the books but are not quite in the same league with organized criminal pursuits such as the drug trade.

Employee theft

It has always been true that workers have received part of their wage in kind. In addition to openly acknowledged or tolerated 'perks', employees invariably find other ways of cheating the boss out of goods, services or cash.[12] The British term for this is 'fiddling', while in the US the less ambiguous term 'employee theft' is usually used. As innocent as some fiddles are, they do involve misappropriation of property, and for this reason writers on the subject have also used phrases such as 'part-time crime' and 'borderline crime'. Stuart Henry introduced his work on the subject as follows:

> This book is about property crimes committed by ordinary people in legitimate jobs. It is about the pilfering and fiddling of goods and services that goes on every day in factories, shops and offices up and down the country . . . It describes how the relationships among 'trading partners' and the flow of goods between them forms a hidden economy within our society.[13]

Fiddles cannot be easily categorized with respect to the law. A report published by the Outer Circle Policy Group, a private organization which has extensively studied the phenomenon, put it well: 'The margin between legal and illegal is shadowy, between legitimate and illegitimate even more so. Old perks are redefined as theft, new perks are redesigned to avoid new forms of taxation.'[14]

The practices which might be included under fiddles are varied enough so that considering the whole phenomenon a form of crime is misleading. Often the distinction between a perk and a fiddle is quite vague; employers may tolerate a degree of cheating but will crack down once it has passed some unspecified point. Most of the practices, except substantial embezzlement or theft of goods, rarely lead to criminal charges.

Fiddles might be considered a part of the underground economy because of the unreported and untaxed incomes, in cash or in kind, that employees gain by engaging in such practices. The Central Statistical Office of the UK has taken this position.[15] Yet there is an important difference between fiddles, which involve private diversion of resources used in legitimate business, and off-the-books work, which involves the concealment of productive activities from the government.

Fiddles are perhaps best viewed as a covert form of struggle by workers. These practices, whether engaged in by employees as individuals or in groups, amount to an effort to supplement official wage rates with secret appropriation of goods, services and sometimes cash. One writer on the subject has argued that access to fiddles has in some situations become so customary that workers have gone on strike when those opportunities were eliminated.[16]

The relationship of fiddles to workplace struggles is seen even more clearly in the attempts of some zealous crusaders against employee theft in the US to extend their notion of theft to time on the job. The idea is that all time during the working day belongs to the boss, and an employee who fails to toil at maximum productivity is guilty of stealing time. A study performed by a New York company somehow estimated that 'time theft' cost American companies as much as $125 billion in lost output in 1982. According to a newspaper account:

> The most frequently cited examples of 'time-wasting',
> according to the survey, included coming to work late;
> leaving early; making personal calls on the job; deliberately
> slowing the work-pace to increase overtime; socializing with
> co-workers; stretching lunch hours and coffee breaks; and
> day-dreaming.[17]

It is hard to decide whether to laugh or to be frightened by the notion of 'time theft'. But it is clear that business regards the intensity of the working day as a serious matter and has begun to employ new weapons in this age-old battle. The introduction of computers into more and more workplaces is making possible greater surveillance of workers and may be inhibiting 'time theft'; computerization may also reduce opportunities for other kinds of fiddles.[18] But there is always another side to the story; the computers also give some workers opportunities for stealing from the boss by electronic means.

Cigarette smuggling

State governments in the US impose several forms of excise tax, the most important of which, in terms of revenues, is that levied on the sale of cigarettes. Beginning in the late 1960s, the differential between the tax rates in various states grew great enough to make it profitable for people to buy quantities of cigarettes in one state and resell them in another (through retailers who were willing to overlook the absence of the appropriate tax stamps on the merchandise).

The classic pattern involved purchase in North Carolina, which until 1969 had no excise tax at all on tobacco, and resale in New York City. In the mid-1970s, a truckload of cigarettes sold in this manner yielded a profit of $66,000.[19] One study estimated the total income from this practice at $100 to $170 million in the US in 1975.[20] By the end of the decade, the growth of the smuggling was stemmed by the narrowing of differentials in state tax rates and by a 1978 law which made the practice a federal crime.

On the one hand, cigarette smuggling is akin to criminal activities such as the drug trade, since the act of transporting the merchandise is illegal and has been dominated by large-scale mafia operators. On the other hand, it resembles mere off-the-books activity, since the cigarettes themselves are not illegal and what is essentially involved is tax evasion. A variation of the practice, in which the cigarettes are initially stolen, rather than purchased, in the low-tax state and then sold with counterfeit tax stamps in the high-tax state, does tip the scale in the direction of the criminal side. Yet in general the practice inhabits the gray area between the underground and criminal sectors.

Piracy

Throughout the world these days, many of the best selling and most profitable commodities are cultural products and brand-name goods. There is tremendous demand everywhere for record albums, audio tapes and video-cassettes as well as clothing and jewelry produced by European designers such as Gucci, Louis Vuitton, Hermès and Cartier. Jeans with labels from Levi-Strauss and other famous makers are sought much more eagerly than non-name varieties.

The legitimate manufacturers of these products protect their markets through copyright laws and licensing agreements. Yet the high prices the goods command in relation to their cost of production create tremendous incentives for unauthorized boot-leggers and imitators. The production and sale of counterfeit goods is an immense business that takes place all over the world.[21]

One of the main targets is the entertainment area. Records, tapes and videos are easily reproduced and can be sold at an enormous profit. The music industry puts the sale of unauthorized records and tapes at hundreds of millions of dollars worldwide. Video-cassette piracy is growing rapidly as more and more households acquire video players. The underground video business is centered in London and generates sales of about £100 million a year in the UK alone, according to one estimate.[22] Another developing area is the piracy of computer software. Unauthorized copying of programs already takes place widely among individuals for personal use, but there are signs that a bootleg industry is on the rise.

The appeal of designer labels to consumers of even modest means has given rise to a sizeable counterfeit component in the clothing and jewelry industries. In a number of countries – Taiwan and Italy are among the more notorious – unlicensed production of high-fashion items takes place on a massive scale.[23] In addition to items such as watches and scarves, the counterfeiters produce copies of relatively mundane products such as hair tonic and auto parts. The more sophisticated operators turn out ersatz Apple Computers that are difficult to distinguish from the real thing.

Given that pirates operate in violation of international copyrights and trademarks, their business tends to be carried out in a rather clandestine manner. Most probably do not pay taxes and do not adhere to other government regulations. Yet the extent to which piracy can be considered an outright criminal activity is unclear. In some countries, where the government does not respect foreign copyrights and trademarks, the production of counterfeits may not be in violation of local law at all. Otherwise, as with cigarette smuggling, the products that are being sold through 'gray markets' are not themselves illegal. Piracy resembles underground activity in that some kind of surreptitious production is taking place in order to evade government regulations; in the latter sense the violations occur primarily with regard to the tax laws, while in the former, copyrights and trademarks are what is violated.

These various examples of profit-oriented activity that share characteristics of both the informal and the illegal economies suggest that there may indeed be no clear dividing line between the two. The ways in which one may break the law in the course of earning money are numerous. While there remain important differences between off-the-books work and large-scale drug dealing, the best way to dispose of the legality question is to conclude that there is a continuum of lawbreaking activities ranging from the receipt of small amounts of unreported income to participation in a mafia heroin operation. The underground cannot be strictly separated from the underworld.

6. The government's dilemma

The underground economy is a realm of activity aimed at escaping the inspection and interference of the state. Through the evasion of taxes and the violation of labor laws and other regulations, the informal sector becomes a sort of outlaw economy. The state, which in recent decades has tended to intervene in economic relations, and sometimes supplant the role of private capital, is absent, replaced by more of a nineteenth-century arrangement. Employers and employees confront one another directly, without the legal framework that unions and liberal or social-democratic policies have created for the regular economy. Each party enjoys some, though usually unequal, benefit as a result of denying the state a share of the income deriving from productive activity.

The growth of the informal sector over the past decade has posed a challenge to political leaders of both the Right and the Left. First of all, the phenomenon has thrown into question conventional thinking about the performance of the economy these past years. Conservatively-inclined analysts of the underground claim that the existence of a large amount of unofficial economic activity suggests that the crisis was not at all as serious as everyone thought; stagnation was largely a statistical illusion. On the other side, there are those who argue that the extent to which people had to resort to off-the-books work to supplement regular employment or government benefits – or as the sole means of support – indicated that the effects of unemployment, inflation and fiscal austerity were more severe than previous analyses had concluded.

Whatever the true implication of the underground economy, its existence forces government to make difficult political choices about how to deal with it. Since working and trading off the books thwart fiscal and regulatory policies, one impulse on the part of government has been to see the phenomenon as a disease that has to be eradicated. Legislators and government officials have devised new ways of detecting and discouraging tax evasion and other forms of cheating.

Yet there are many politicians who recognize that cracking down on the informal economy might not be the wisest course of action at a time when the regular economy remains in such a precarious condition. Off-the-books work has often been depicted as a cushion without which the masses of the unemployed might rise up in revolt.

The conflict between enforcement and tolerance has been most pronounced in countries such as the US and Britain where politicians came to power celebrating unregulated capitalism. Reagan, Thatcher and the officials working for them were most acutely caught in the dilemma of needing to collect revenues yet confronting growing numbers of citizens who seemed to take their talk of minimal government seriously enough to cease paying taxes.

From voluntary compliance to *1984*

For years, observers of the US tax systems proudly declared that the so-called voluntary compliance system was overwhelmingly successful. Americans were said to accept their tax burden gracefully, calculating it honestly and paying what might be due at the end of the year with a minimum of delay. This version of the story was, of course, less than completely accurate. It is true that compliance levels were quite high, but that was no surprise, given that since 1943 wages and salaries – by far the largest component of income – were subject to withholding, i.e. taxes were deducted from paychecks. Under-reporting of income in that situation was not possible. The opportunity for reducing one's tax burden came when it was time to tally up the deductions that were permitted from the amount of one's income subject to the statutory rates. The trick was to compile enough deductions – medical expenses, interest payments, costs of earning income, etc. – not only to avoid an additional payment at filing time, but also to get a refund from what had been paid out over the course of the year.

This practice is generally legal and goes under the name of tax avoidance, as opposed to evasion. In fact, the opportunities for avoidance are very much taken into account when Congress enacts changes in the tax code. Even more than through public spending, the federal government has used the tax aspect of fiscal policy to achieve its social and economic aims. The code has been strewn with all sorts of provisions that are supposed to create incentives or disincentives for various kinds of activity by individuals and businesses.

To be sure that taxpayers are merely taking advantage of the code and not violating it, the Internal Revenue Service has one of the largest staffs of any federal agency outside of the military – some 85,000 people. Its annual budget is in the area of $3 billion. The task of the agency is indeed awesome. It processes more than 170 million returns a year, of which 135 million are for income tax and 95 million of those are from individuals. It must scan all those returns for mathematical accuracy, audit those with suspicious entries and carry out criminal investigations of major violators.

Despite the monumental efforts of the IRS, people attracted to the underground economy in the 1970s did find ways to conceal income. Many simply never filed a tax return. The General Accounting Office, an investigative arm of Congress, estimated in a 1979 report that about five million individuals and couples had chosen this route. They had taxable income of about $30 billion and tax liabilities of some $2 billion.[1]

The decision not to file a return when working *on* the books means taking the chance that the IRS will not detect that income through its program of document matching. All businesses and other institutions making substantial payments to individuals are supposed to report that fact to the IRS. For many years the large majority of those forms simply collected dust in IRS offices. The agency was not able to check that each of those bits of income had been faithfully recorded on people's returns. By the mid-1970s more and more of these reports from large institutions were being submitted to the IRS on computer tape, making matching much more feasible. Yet it is likely that much of the income that people were not reporting had been earned from smaller businesses that still sent their documents to the IRS on paper, thereby reducing the chances that matching would be done and undeclared income discovered.

Moreover, this form of income under-reporting is only a limited part of the universe of underground activity. It is extremely difficult for the IRS to detect unreported income for which no documents exist. This can only be done when someone, such as a gangster, is living a conspicuously lavish life without the official income to support it. In this way, the IRS prosecuted Al Capone in 1929 when other law enforcement agencies failed to gather enough direct evidence to convict him on other than fiscal crimes.

With the spread of the underground economy, the IRS got tougher. It began seeking new ways to discover people whose standard of living was out of line with their official income. In the past this would have required an army of informers; but in this age of technology computers can be called on to be the spies.

In 1983 the IRS approached a number of private companies that were in the business of compiling profiles of the spending habits of the population. Using public data such as property records and automobile registrations, these firms have assembled income estimates for large samples of individuals. The IRS wanted to purchase these computerized profiles and compare them with its own records to detect possible tax evaders. Several of the companies refused to supply the data but in late 1983 the IRS found a firm that was willing to do so, and the agency started a pilot project in four states.[2]

Although the IRS plan was unique in its use of privately collected data, the use of computers to detect cheating committed against the government has been on the rise since the mid 1970s. State and local governments as well as federal agencies have used computer matches to search for people who may have been improperly receiving unemployment compensation or some other benefit while appearing on a regular payroll. The IRS has advanced these practices to a new level of sophistication with its plans to establish direct electronic links with local government records. The growing centralization of computer files has begun to be recognized as a threat to civil liberties. An implication of the controversy is that there is a political limit on the extent to which the IRS can fight tax evasion. With enough computers and rewards for informers (such bounties already exist) it is theoretically possible for the state to learn of every transaction. Yet the results of that would be a vastly more oppressive climate: the tax collector's *1984*.

In Britain, Inland Revenue has not yet reached the point for its enforcement methods to raise comparable concern about violations of privacy. Yet things are moving in that direction. In 1983 a parliamentary committee headed by Lord Keith issued an exhaustive study on tax compliance that called for much tougher policies on the part of Inland Revenue and the Board of Customs and Excise (which collects VAT). Calling many of the existing collection practices 'antediluvian', the Keith report recommended more rigorous record-keeping requirements for taxpayers, publication of the names of evaders, and random audits of taxpayers' accounts. The committee implied that the measures might require the adoption of a system more like that of the US, in which all taxpayers (except those with minimal incomes) file annual returns in addition to making payments throughout the year.[3]

At the same time, Inland Revenue has been modernizing its procedures. In October 1983 it initiated a pilot program for the computerization of pay-as-you-earn operations, and after overcoming the objections of the staff federation, the agency announced in July 1984 that the new technology would be introduced throughout the country. Inland Revenue's staff, which stood at about 70,000 in 1984, has declined in the Thatcher years but the number of investigators has increased. According to the agency's 1983 report, the experimental deployment of 70 investigators in local tax offices to seek out people working off the books was successful. About £200 million in tax due on undeclared income was recovered in 1983. Plans were accordingly made to deploy an additional 850 investigators in the period from 1984 to 1988.[4]

Back in the US, the Internal Revenue Service has been considering another novel way of dealing with unreported income that may or may not raise civil liberties problems. The agency was persuaded by the evidence that a substantial part of tax evasion occurs through cash transactions involving large-denomination bills. As noted in an earlier chapter, the big bill phenomenon helped lead economists in the US to the discovery of the underground economy. James Henry, who was primarily responsible for making the link, argued that the government could seriously deter major underground transactions by instituting a recall of $50 and $100 bills.[5]

As envisioned by Henry, the Treasury would suddenly announce one day that the big bills were no longer valid and would have to be exchanged for smaller denomination notes at banks. Those exchanges would take place under the supervision of the IRS, and anyone who had turned in a large number of big bills could end up being investigated. The recall would amount to a one-time assault on the cash assets of organized crime and major tax evaders who had been hoarding currency in large denominations. The assumption was that once the recall had been completed, illicit transactions would become much more cumbersome, since the use of small denomination notes would require cash shipments of much greater volume. For large drug deals in particular this could create major logistical difficulties. It would do nothing, however, to inhibit off-the-books transactions involving smaller notes.

Although Henry's proposal was not taken seriously when published in 1976, the IRS later found it appealing. According to press reports in 1982, the agency had included the recall among a 'wish list' of proposals it submitted to the Treasury Department (of which the IRS is a part).[6] The agency's wish was not granted, but in the light of recent publicity surrounding cash laundering and other illicit movements of large amounts of currency, it is possible that the scheme may surface again. In fact, recalls have been carried out in recent years in countries such as India (see chapter 8), Israel and Nigeria.[7]

The underground and the supply side

Not everyone in government is as zealous as the IRS and its foreign counterparts in attacking the underground economy. First of all, there are those who recognize that there are probably not enough jobs in the regular economy to employ those who are currently working exclusively in the informal sector. In other words, the underground economy has been serving as a kind of cushion against the full impact of the crisis in the above-ground economy. To eliminate those jobs – since most of them would evaporate if subjected to full taxation and regulation – would mean to swell the ranks of the unemployed and potentially contribute to social unrest. There has been a reluctance on the part of most politicians to publicly acknowledge this idea, though a 1980 report submitted to the EEC called informal work a social 'safety valve' and warned governments against suppressing the phenomenon too strongly.[8]

Since the start of the Reagan Administration, the US government's position on the underground economy has been ambiguous. The IRS, of course, has passionately pursued its bureaucratic mandate of collecting all the taxes stipulated by law. Yet Reagan himself has taken a more tolerant view of the phenomenon. In an April 1982 radio address he jocularly referred to informal sector participants as 'a growing group of citizens who've already given themselves a tax cut . . . The people in this [underground] economy are, I'm sure, honest people in most of their activities; they just have a double standard where taxes are concerned.' He concluded on a wistful note: 'As we struggle to trim government spending, it's hard not to think of how close that unpaid tax could come to wiping out the deficit.'[9]

Reagan returned to this theme in his January 1984 State of the Union Address. He suggested it was up to government to reform the tax code in a way that 'could result in that underground economy being brought into the sunlight of honest tax compliance.'[10] The image is of well-meaning businessmen and professionals who simply cannot survive the burden of taxes and regulations. If the government did enough to relieve those burdens – and Reagan was clearly repeating his claim that he had done what he could but Congress stood in the way of additional reform – the underground entrepreneur would be happy to conform with the law.

The decision about how to deal with the informal sector is straightforward for liberal or social democratic regimes. Since those political approaches rely on the state to deal with social and economic problems, any attempt to circumvent government oversight and regulation must be suppressed. Yet for conservatives such as Reagan and Thatcher, there are more mixed feelings. The underground economy does have its appealing points.

Ronald Reagan came to power in 1980 riding a wave of discontent with the federal government in the US. He represented an unusual fusion of traditional conservative ideology (corporate Republicanism) with a new form of right-wing populism. The major influence on Reagan's economic thinking, at least at the beginning of his administration, came from the latter camp. Beginning in the late 1970s an eclectic group of advisers put together an economic perspective that came to be known as supply-side economics. In part, the ideology underlying the theory was little more than a rehash of the right-wing libertarian views of Milton Friedman and Friedrich Von Hayek. Complete and undying faith was placed in the free market while government was seen as essentially evil and truly useful only for organizing the police and the military and regulating the money supply. The supply-siders, however, were most obsessed with taxes. They saw high tax levies as sapping the life of society by weakening the motivation of men to work and support a family (in which women were supposed to be full-time housewives).

The case they made for massive tax cuts was economic as well as moral. The supply-siders in effect appropriated one part of Keynesian fiscal theory and put it in a very different political context. Keynes' original theory was, to put it simply, based on the idea that either a rise in government spending or a decline in tax rates would have a stimulative effect on the economy by raising the demand for goods produced by the private sector. The supply-siders chose to see the benefit of tax cuts (but not spending increases) in the incentive they gave people to make additional investments and work more hours in the knowledge that government was going to appropriate less of the additional income which resulted.

Most often the supply-siders argued that the effect of the tax burden and excessive government regulation was simply to encourage people to invest less and work shorter hours (they insist on believing that workers can themselves decide how many hours to spend on the job). But at times they acknowledged that people had responded to those weights by taking their business underground. George Gilder, one of the gurus of this world view, wrote: 'As families break down under the pressure of taxes and welfare, moral constraints tend to dissolve . . . and the temptations grow for concealed and undocumented income.'[11] This declaration was in line with Reagan's statement that there were good reasons for people to choose to evade taxes and regulations but the process of doing so was, because it broke the law, immoral. The supply-siders would apparently have preferred that the victims of liberalism simply devoted their energies to getting the Right into power sooner, rather than taking matters into their own hands and becoming economic outlaws. The proper thing to do was to support large official tax cuts, not granting 100 per cent reductions to oneself.

Meanwhile in Britain, a politician with similar views had come to power. Margaret Thatcher's inspiration was perhaps a more orthodox reading of Von Hayek and Friedman, by way of Tory thinkers Keith Joseph and Geoffrey Howe. The British version of the new laissez-faire put more emphasis on monetarism than tax relief in its economic policy. Yet tax cuts were seen as important as well. Howe sounded very much like a supply-sider when he declared in a July 1979 speech that the tax system 'has come to represent a major impediment to initiative, innovation and risk-taking'.[12] As in the US, the tax cuts were also supposed to reduce the motivation for people to enter the informal economy.

Given their ideological bias, it is likely that the new generation of British and American conservatives had some sympathy for individuals who had found a way of circumventing bothersome state policies. Yet once these politicians took office they were faced with the practical problems of conducting economic policy. No matter what their ultimate intentions, the Tories could not suddenly dispense with taxes and regulation altogether. Most pressing was the need to reduce budget deficits.

It is in the area of deficits that the conservatives faced the greatest conflict between their desire to cut taxes and their need to practise fiscal responsibility. In the US the supply-siders had at first theorized away the problem with the simplistic device of the Laffer curve. Invented by an economist at the University of Southern California named Arthur Laffer, the curve represented the notion that as tax rates were increased, the revenues generated by those rates eventually reached a point of diminishing returns. Beyond that point people, disgruntled with the share taken by the state, would start reducing the amount of income-generating activity they engaged in. With a shrinking tax base, the revenues received by government would steadily decline. Laffer and his disciples argued that the US was reaching that critical turning point and therefore needed substantial tax cuts.[13]

The crusade was taken up by Reagan in his 1980 campaign, and after being elected he got Congress to go along with a tax bill that cut personal rates by nearly 25 per cent over three years and liberalized business levies to the point that the press began to speak of 'the quiet repeal of the corporate income tax'.[14] Though Reagan eventually ended up enjoying the effects of a cyclical upturn in the economy, the supply-side boom never happened. Revenues from an increased level of business did not offset the massive losses to the Treasury from the 1981 bill. This, combined with the rapid increases in military spending, generated the largest budget deficits in US history. Nor did the tax cuts induce many people to abandon their habits of avoidance and evasion. The tax shelter business continued to prosper, and there were no signs that participants in the underground were emerging 'into the sunlight of honest tax compliance' in great numbers.

The third world amid the first

Despite the shortcomings of economic policy in both the US and the UK, the conservatives running the governments in both countries remained committed to the doctrine of interfering as little as possible with the free market. For practical and political reasons this could not mean explicit support for the uncontrolled business of the informal sector. Yet the Tories did find ways to promote some of the appealing (to them) features of the informal economy in quasi-underground business arrangements.

The first of these was the enterprise zone scheme.[15] The zone idea was first put forth in Britain in the late 1970s by Peter Hall, a professor of urban planning at Reading University. Although a Fabian socialist, Hall was impressed with the fast-growing economies of laissez-faire Hong Kong and other bastions of free enterprise. He decided that unfettered capitalism was the solution to economic development in the first world as well as the third. Hall found a supporter in Geoffrey Howe, and after the latter became Chancellor of the Exchequer in Margaret Thatcher's first government, he began pushing for an enterprise zone experiment.

In Hall's original conception, the zones were supposed to be designated areas where a wide range of labor laws, taxes and other government regulations were simply suspended. When the

Thatcher government did institute about a dozen zones in blighted urban areas around the UK, political pressures forced her to limit the provisions to a few concessions such as elimination of property taxes, 100 per cent capital allowance, and simplified bureaucratic procedures. Nevertheless, the plan was denounced by the Left as a step toward restoring nineteenth-century work conditions.[16]

Some advocates of a nineteenth-century revival in the US adopted the enterprise zone idea at about the same time, amid the heated discussion over the future of devastated urban areas such as the South Bronx in New York. While President Carter's uninspiring urban policy proposals languished in Congress, conservatives, who had started mobilizing in a serious way, offered the scheme as a bold new approach to solving the crisis of the cities. The plan was pushed by the ultra-right Heritage Foundation and its staff member Stuart Butler. In a 1980 essay Butler said the zones would 'provide an attractive climate for private money and business'. Among the appealing features, he listed reduced taxes, eased zoning rules and the possible elimination of rent control and the minimum wage.[17]

Butler continued his crusade, which was endorsed by presidential candidate Reagan, in the pages of *Policy Review*, the house organ of Heritage. He argued that the depopulation and economic stagnation of older cities were often the result of misguided government policies. 'The chief barrier to the revival of dilapidated inner-city districts is not the lack of government intervention but all too often the presence of it', Butler argued, and he urged that free enterprise be given a chance to deal with the problem.[18]

If the enterprise zone idea held any appeal for the residents of depressed urban areas, it was the possibility that the scheme might provide them with some sort of decent job. Yet the discussion of the zones by their proponents suggested that the jobs to be created would not be the kind that ensure rapid ascent up the ladder of success. The attempt to eliminate minimum wage levels in the zones suggested that the jobs would be quite low-paying and undoubtedly insecure and non-union. This was the implication of Butler's vision, as stated by the *New York Times*, of 'dozens of "basement businesses" – laundries, garment shops, bakeries and the like – each employing a half-dozen or so unskilled workers'.[19]

This suggests that the zones are meant to play a part in the restructuring of labor markets and forms of production being promoted by some governments in response to the crisis of the regular economy. They hope to reverse mainstream industrial decline by encouraging marginal industry. Work in substandard conditions serves as a form of social control for people thrown out of their jobs in the abandoned large factories. In line with the fiscal austerity promoted since the mid-1970s, it is deemed better to keep people in precarious employment than to grant their subsistence through social spending.

The zone proposal pursued this aim with precedents from the third world, where capital has been much bolder in its experiments in controlling labor. In a sense all of Puerto Rico was made an enterprise zone after the Second World War through Operation Bootstrap. An analogous scheme, the Border Industrialization Program, was instituted in northern Mexico following the end of the Bracero, or guest worker, system in 1965. Since the early 1960s dozens of third world countries, especially in Asia, have created export-processing zones, in which foreign investors, mainly from the US and West Germany, have been able to take advantage of cheap and strictly-managed labor in assembly operations that had been shifted out of factories in the advanced countries. It was not surprising that the *Washington Post* said that 'the ideal behind the urban enterprise zone is to help the nation's blighted central cities follow the developmental trail blazed by the industrializing countries of Asia'.[20]

It is true that the conservatives pushing enterprise zones in Britain and the US have not yet been able to realize fully their third-world dream. In the US, zone proponents were never able to garner enough support in Congress to pass a federal program. Many state and local governments, however, went ahead and established moderate versions of the zones on their own.[21] Meanwhile in Britain, the Thatcher government did expand the number of zones to more than two dozen, yet there was little evidence that the scheme was doing much to create new jobs. In addition, it turned out that whatever success these outposts of free enterprise attained required a substantial degree of public spending and intervention. Government bodies have spent millions of pounds in assembling the sites, providing infrastructure, and promoting the zones.[22]

The irony of this situation has been ignored by the Tories in their rush to aid business. In fact, in early 1984 the Thatcher government announced that it would move ahead with a related plan for the establishment of freeports. These would be zones in which firms could import goods and assemble them into finished products for re-export without paying customs duties.[23]

The freeports, like enterprise zones, were initially proposed by the Right (in the case of freeports, the Adam Smith Institute) in a more extreme version. Political considerations forced the government to adopt modified versions of the plans, with some of the more controversial elements eliminated. This does not mean that the creation of these zones has lost its sinister implications. The Right continues to press for more drastic removal of state regulation, and the establishment of any sort of zone aids their crusade.

If the more extreme forms of the zones come into existence, the third-world precedents would be applied with full force. Employers could be given a completely free hand in the treatment of labor as workplace rights and protections were swept away. Local authorities could play little more than a symbolic role, with real political power held by entrepreneurs. At this point, the zones would resemble the conditions that are already in existence in the more exploitative aspects of the informal economy. In their worst incarnation, the zones could thus be seen either as state-sanctioned underground business or the introduction of more oppressive conditions into enterprises that are above-ground.

Precariousness hits home

Along with pushing its crusade for special zones, the Right in both Britain and the US has been chipping away at worker protection. Apart from a general weakening of labor law enforcement through the appointment of conservatives to the Labor Department and the National Labor Relations Board, the Reagan Administration targeted several groups of workers who were most dependent on small businesses for employment. The first of these was the young.

Since the mid-1970s policymakers throughout the developed world have been preoccupied with the problem of youth unemployment. Whereas liberals saw the solution in job training programs and public employment projects, the new generation of conservatives in the US had a different view. They argued that young people were without jobs because the minimum wage laws priced them out of the labor market; the supposedly low productivity of young workers simply made it unprofitable for employers to hire them at $2.30 an hour (in 1977; $3.35 in 1984). The conservatives (and some liberals) proposed either to eliminate the minimum wage for young workers altogether or at least set a lower floor for them. One conservative black economist went so far as to call the minimum wage 'racist' because it deprived young blacks of the right to sell their labor at whatever price the market had set.[24]

The Reagan Administration took up the call for a subminimum 'teenwage'. Reagan himself linked a statement of his position on the matter with a nostalgic recollection of his own low-paid early employment experience:

> There weren't any government programs that made the employer have to hire an auditor and deduct from my paycheck for Social Security or other programs of that kind. He could just reach into his pocket every week and count out what he owed me and hand it to me in cash [off the books?], and I wouldn't give up that experience I had for anything in the world.[25]

Organized labor and its supporters in Congress had a less rosy view of the past and effectively blocked the administration's teenwage plan. Reagan's Labor Department did, however, carry out administrative changes that allowed low-wage employers to make greater use of very young workers. In 1982 child labor restrictions were eased for 14- and 15-year olds, allowing them to work longer hours during a school week.

A second group of workers targeted in Reagan's erosion of labor protection were women, and this was done through an attempt to weaken laws concerning home labor. Earlier in the century, home labor performed by women under extremely exploitative conditions was common in a number of light industries, especially clothing. The 1938 Fair Labor Standards Act and subsequent federal actions banned home work entirely in seven industries in which conditions had been worst. For years home work ceased to be an issue as the practice steadily disappeared.

But by the late 1970s, with the spread of marginal labor of all sorts, home labor made a comeback. During the last year of the Carter Administration some employers of home labor for knitting ski-caps in Vermont challenged the law, claiming it should not apply in a rural area where it simply was not practical for people to travel long distances to work in a factory. Besides, the companies claimed that the home workers were well paid and toiled in decent conditions.

While the Carter Administration insisted on enforcing the law, the Reagan Labor Department saw the case as one of small businesses struggling against an irrational government regulation. Yet Labor Secretary Ray Donovan did not simply amend the rules to legalize the situation in Vermont. In May 1981 he proposed eliminating *all* restrictions on home labor in urban and rural areas. This prompted an outcry from organized labor and liberals, and several months later, Donovan relented and limited the change to the Vermont situation.[26] Even at that, a federal appeals court ruled in November 1983 that that action was illegal and reinstituted the complete ban in the seven industries. The Labor Department then looked for ways to have the law changed.

The rise of the entrepreneur

The enterprise zone plan and the attempted dismantling of labor standards were consistent with the general glorification of entrepreneurship and laissez-faire in the new conservative creed. The attitude was elevated to the height of absurdity by supply-side philosopher George Gilder. According to him, capitalist invest-ments are actually 'gifts' that the entrepreneur makes to society without knowing what, if anything, he will receive in return:

The gifts will succeed only to the extent that they are altruistic and spring from an understanding of the needs of others. They depend on faith in an essentially fair and responsive humanity. In such a world, one can give without a contract of compensation. One can venture without the assurance of reward. One can seek the surprises of profit, rather than the more limited benefits of contractual pay.[27]

Even in less extreme form, the cult of entrepreneurship has been enjoying a wide popularity, in Britain as well as the US. The failure of macroeconomic policies on both sides of the Atlantic has prompted a revived faith in small business as the catalyst of a new round of economic growth. The magic of Silicon Valley, for instance, has even impressed some observers on the Left. At the end of 1983, *Mother Jones* magazine published a highly favorable profile of electronics industry entrepreneurs. While acknowledging some of the nagging questions about how these high-tech businessmen treated their production workers, the entrepreneurs were celebrated as 'the new American heroes' for their contributions to innovation and economic growth.[28]

It is not the case that everyone has embraced a thoroughly 'small is beautiful' doctrine for the future of capitalism. Conservative governments have devoted most of their energies to helping big business rather than small-time operators. And many of the celebrated entrepreneurs head companies with revenue of tens or hundreds of millions of dollars a year. In addition, many of the small companies that have prospered are dependent on big business through subcontracting relationships.

Aside from being an ideological ploy, the interest in small businesses in enterprise zones and elsewhere is linked more to the need to find something to do with the growing numbers of people who are made redundant by the transformation of the mainstream economy. This is quite apparent in Britain, where the Thatcher government has instituted a plan to turn unemployed workers into entrepreneurs. The Enterprise Allowance Scheme was initiated by the Manpower Services Commission in 1982. It allowed redundant workers to continue collecting £40 a week in unemployment compensation for up to a year while they started up their own businesses. The plan was not meant for everyone: to qualify one had to have at least £1000 to invest in the venture. By early 1984 about 26,000 people were enrolled in the plan but it was too early to determine how successful these new entrepreneurs were and how many may have been forced to take their businesses underground.[29]

The underground dilemma for policymakers

The existence of a substantial underground sector is also indirectly used by some conservative politicians to deflect criticism of their handling of the economy as a whole. The discovery of a vast realm of production, employment and additional income has served as a basis for claiming that there really has not been rising unemployment, declining productivity, poor GNP growth, and stagnant real income. Peter Gutmann, who more or less started the debate in the US, has used his discovery to argue that liberal policies were totally misguided. He wrote in 1979:

> The Administration's fight against inflation has been unsuccessful because it is based on an illusion: the government perceives the unemployment rate – quite inaccurately – as high. This illusion has come to control the reality of federal policies, long precluding effective policies to counter inflation.[30]

Carl Simon and Ann Witte, authors of *Beating the System: the Underground Economy*, have stated that 'the systematic biases in recorded statistics which fail to take into account the underground economy lead to misguided (and probably overstimulatory) public policy decisions'.[31]

The policies of Reagan and Thatcher have been far from overstimulatory and have not betrayed an excessive concern with the problem of unemployment. The undying faith they placed in the free market at a time when the regular economy was deep in crisis could be interpreted in part as a tolerance for activities that are off the books. Through enterprise zones and other measures fostering marginal production, conservative policies have both helped control a surplus population generated by the crisis of big business and aided an expansion of capital accumulation by small entrepreneurs.

It is likely that politicians everywhere will continue to be confused as to how to regard the underground economy: whether to see it as an outlaw realm that has to be suppressed or as a heartening expansion of unfettered business activity. This is a problem of legitimacy as well as economic policy. The decision to take productive activity underground is a challenge to the capitalist state, whether in its conservative or liberal/social-democratic incarnation.

Liberal/social-democratic governments face the difficulty of reconciling their commitment to planning and state intervention with a growing inclination on the part of people to take economic matters into their own hands. Even policies promising full employment and restored social services may have little appeal for those who have had a taste of the more lucrative side of the underground.

The problem for the conservative state is that of finding a policy that gives free enough rein to the outlaw entrepreneurs without letting things get so anarchic that underground employees begin to organize to fight brutal conditions. It is a strange kind of economic management that this kind of state must exercise with regard to the informal sector. It is no longer a matter of deciding how much control to exercise but how little.

Whatever the ruling policies are, government officials are bound to have a love-hate relationship with the underground economy. Until now the degree to which governments have overtly demonstrated each of those feelings has not been intense. But if the crisis of the regular economy is not resolved in some convincing fashion, the informal sector may come to be used by politicians in more explicit and direct ways. An intensified campaign against the underground might be exploited as a convenient diversion of attention away from the problems of the economic mainstream. An even more sinister possibility is that governments could try to 'colonize' the underground and use it as a place for keeping the superfluous workforce 'on ice' permanently. Rather than being, as now, a realm in which greater freedom and flexibility for people is at least possible, a government-sanctioned underground – an extreme form of enterprise zones – would be unambiguously oppressive.

7. The submerged economy in Italy

If there were an Olympic competition for informal production and tax evasion, Italy would capture all the gold medals. Decentralization of industry, the revival of home work and child labor, and other phenomena that go against the grain of modern economic development appeared first in Italy and remain more pervasive there than anywhere else in Europe and North America.[1] The peculiarities of the Italian economy were once considered symptomatic of a relatively backward country, but by the late 1970s it became clear that Italy was, on the contrary, in the vanguard of a transformation that was spreading throughout the capitalist world.

The existence of a large and growing *economia sommersa* ('submerged economy') has been a major fact of Italian life since the early 1970s. Estimates of the population doing *lavoro nero* (black or off-the-books work) exclusively have gone as high as five million, compared to an official labor force of some 20 million, and at least ten per cent of that latter figure are believed to engage in *doppio lavoro* (moonlighting) that is invariably underground.[2] Italian economists have been more reluctant to make underground GNP estimates than their counterparts in the US and Britain, but those who have done so have settled on a figure of about 30 per cent of official national output.[3] In 1979 bowing to political pressure, the Italian central statistical agency, ISTAT, went back and revised all of the country's national accounts for the previous two decades, adjusting everything upward about eight per cent to reflect unmeasured economic activity. The process is known to have scandalized officials of the International Monetary Fund, which had extended substantial loans to the Italian government and could not countenance such a cavalier manipulation of sacred statistics. But in Italy it was widely agreed that

ISTAT had not done enough to bring the official figures in line with reality.

From the economic miracle to the sweatshop

It was an apparent anomaly in official statistics that led Italian analysts to the discovery of the underground economy in the first place. While in the US this realization was related to the surprisingly high levels of currency in circulation, the Italian path led from the data on labor force participation. Back in the late 1960s, Italian economists and sociologists were wondering why, in a country which had experienced one of the most rapid rates of growth in the early postwar period, the percentage of the population in the labor force was so much lower than in other industrial nations. After spending some time on conventional explanations (for example, that rising 'affluence' made supposedly supplementary wage-earning by wives unnecessary), analysts began to see that there was much employment that was simply not reflected in the official figures.[4] A great deal of this work was being done by women who did not describe themselves as employed when responding to government surveys. This was because they did not want to jeopardize their husband's family allowance payments or because they regarded themselves primarily as housewives.

The non-worker sense of identity was fostered by the fact that the work was being done in unusual circumstances. Unlike the typical Italian worker – a full-time employee of a large corporation – these new wage-earners were being employed on odd schedules in tiny workshops not far from where they lived. Often the labor had to be performed in the worker's own home.

These women were the first wave of Italian workers to be swept into a process of industrial transformation in which aspects of production were transferred from large factories to much smaller plants. Business brought about this productive decentralization in a quest for sharply reduced costs and greater flexibility in the use of labor. This deliberate process of restructuring represented the response of capital to the power that workers in large factories had gained through a period of intense struggle. Beginning with the 'hot autumn' strikes and demonstrations of 1969, rank and file workers in the industrial concentrations of the north posed a direct challenge to the authoritarian management techniques and low wages which served as the basis for the Italian economic miracle of the 1950s and early 1960s. The upheaval at Fiat factories in Turin, Pirelli plants around Milan, and the chemical complexes of Porto Marghera south of Venice convinced Italian business that such concentrations of organized and militant workers were too dangerous.[5]

While corporations in countries such as the US initially responded to growing labor strength by shifting investment to non-union parts of the country and low-wage havens in the third world – and only later began decentralizing – the Italian approach from the start was to disperse production, and thereby the labor force, into small factories that were easier to manage and more difficult for labor to organize.[6] The impetus to decentralize was heightened when parliament responded to labor unrest with the passage of the *Statuto dei lavoratori* in 1970. This general labor law provided Italian workers with far more job security than their counterparts in other industrial countries; dismissals became next to impossible. Because the statute did not apply to firms with fewer than 15 employees, the period following its enactment saw the creation of countless enterprises with 14 people on the payroll. In this way businesses were able to circumvent legally the rights and protections that the labor movement had won through both legislative and contract battles. Yet many of the small operations ended up going off the books to avail themselves of complete freedom in their treatment of labor as well as complete evasion of taxes. Thus decentralization of production brought about a major expansion of the underground economy.

The use of the small firm as the pivot of the restructuring process was made easier by the fact that Italy had a lower level of industrial concentration than other advanced countries. Whereas thousands of small operations continued to exist through the 1960s because of the unevenness of Italian economic development, they proliferated in the 1970s in a more dynamic role. The sector of small-scale industry, once scorned as inefficient, became more productive and profitable than its large-scale counterpart, especially the flaccid state-run corporations that were created during the fascist period. In a study of the clothing and textile industries, economist Luigi Frey found that the small firms were achieving, thanks to the use of non-union and unprotected workers, savings in labor costs equal to about 14 per cent of the average output per worker.[7]

The dynamism of the new breed of small firms has not come solely from the super-exploitation of labor; there has also been considerable use of sophisticated machinery and technology. This has happened as metal-working, electronics, and other more capital-intensive industries joined the traditionally more fragmented sectors – clothing, textiles, and leather goods – in the decentralization process.

On the face of it, the proliferation of profitable and often technically advanced small firms flies in the face of both Marxist and orthodox theories of industrial development. Economists of all stripes have placed great emphasis on economy of scale, and Marx seemed to regard concentration of the means of production and centralization of the ownership of capital as essential aspects of accumulation.

What the restructuring of Italian industry in the 1970s represented, however, was not the refutation of these theories but rather the modification of previous patterns as a result of an effort by business to counteract an extraordinary increase in the power of labor. In simple economic terms, Italian analysts have argued that the notion of economy of scale did not necessarily imply anything about the size of the firm or the workplace; it only related to the technical organization of production. Economist Sebastiano Brusco, a leading proponent of this view, has noted that most large factories are simply collections of various small-scale production processes that could just as well be dispersed, assuming that the costs of co-ordination and of transporting intermediate products were outweighed by the savings achieved in the decentralized operations.[8] Many Italian businessmen apparently shared this opinion and made sure the last stipulation held by using precarious labor in the small plants.

There was also the question of how autonomous the new small firms really were. After years of passionate debate, Italian analysts ended up generally agreeing that the decentralized firms were dependent directly or indirectly on large corporations. In some cases this was obvious, since the small firms were exclusively engaged in work subcontracted out by big business. When the small companies did sell finished products directly to consumers, it was usually in market conditions controlled by the more sizeable manufacturers.

This suggests that the decentralization has not been fundamental, that it has not meant a significant decrease in the importance and power of concentrated industrial capital. Many of the small firms, while legally independent, have amounted to little more than external departments of large corporations. It is for this reason that some Italian economists have made use of the phrase *fabbrica diffusa*, or 'diffused factory'.

The political proponents of restructuring have tried to disguise the fact that basic power relations have not changed by promoting the notion that decentralization represents a flowering of entrepreneurship. Endless articles in the Italian press have celebrated the industriousness of the inhabitants of towns such as Carpi and Prato, where extensive textile production takes place in decentralized form.[9] Ideological use of this Italian phenomenon has also been made by the American media. The *New York Times* called Prato one of 'the number of small oases of hard work and business acumen in a country otherwise beset by strikes, industrial inefficiency, and overstaffing'. *Time* magazine has written of the 'mythical small entrepreneur *Sciur* Brambilla (Mr. Brambilla in Milanese dialect) for whom business is business and doing very well. These tireless Brambillas . . . are the men who keep Italy booming despite constant reports of an economy on the brink of bankruptcy. Facing a tough job, *Sciur* Brambilla spits on his calloused hands and goes to it.'[10]

Women and children first

What some observers in Italy or abroad often choose to ignore is that the restructuring of Italian industry has brought with it labor conditions that are reminiscent of nineteenth-century England: working days of 16 hours, abysmal wages often on a piecework basis, an extremely intense pace of production, very dangerous and unhealthy working environments, and the absence of social insurance and job security – in short, 'managerial prerogative' run wild.

The worst abuses of decentralization are usually seen in the most radical form of the phenomenon: the relocation of production into the home of the worker.[11] It was the expansion of unreported home labor that first brought economists to the conclusion that hidden employment was what accounted for the low rates of official labor force participation. In study after study in the early 1970s, it was found that this supposedly outdated form of production was rapidly expanding throughout the country. In addition to sectors such as textiles, clothing and footwear, in which a limited amount of home labor had always existed, more technically sophisticated industries were found to be relocating phases, and sometimes entire cycles, of output in workers' homes. Women in Turin were turning out parts for Fiat subcontractors on basement presses; in the region of Umbria they were fabricating miniature motors for teleprinters; in Prato they were producing cloth that ended up in the prayer mats used by pilgrims in Mecca.

This remarkable form of production was estimated by Frey to involve at least one million women.[12] Despite the absence of pay deductions, wage levels were miserable; researchers in the early 1970s found effective wages as low as the equivalent of 40 cents an hour. Rates were higher for those with better skills and those who toiled more intensively. Home workers were usually compelled to purchase their own equipment and pay (at the higher domestic rate) for the electricity consumed by those machines. This amounted to an enormous saving in costs for the small entrepreneur who made use of home labor. One analysis found that domestic production in the knitwear industry cost only 25 to 40 per cent of equivalent factory output in the same sector.[13]

The arrangement also meant the elimination of virtually all risk for the entrepreneur. He had very little fixed investment and could respond to changes in demand quite quickly. By restricting his activities to buying raw material and selling the finished products, the user of home labor was able to ignore problems related to output (the piecework system took care of that) and focus on the financial and commercial aspects of the business. The home worker was stuck with purchasing and maintaining the means of production and overseeing her own exploitation. Yet she remained controlled by what Marx, in his discussion of nineteenth-century home work, called the 'invisible threads' manipulated by the possessor of capital.[14]

Another aspect of Victorian free enterprise that Italian business rediscovered in the 1970s was child labor. This practice had remained in existence in a few places throughout this century but in the past 15 years it has spread as a notorious form of *lavoro nero* throughout the country. Estimates put the number of underaged illegal workers at about 450,000 with the majority in the south. In the late 1970s researchers Clara de Marco and Manlio Talamo found that nearly one quarter of the children in the Naples region aged 11 to 14 were not enrolled in school, and among those who were, truancy levels were high.[15]

Many of those evaders of compulsory education were clearly working off the books and usually in wretched conditions. Journalistic accounts of the exploitation of children as young as six and seven in Naples matched the reports of the British factory inspectors 140 years earlier. Dangerous conditions in basement workshops have brought about numerous tragedies. One of the worst occurred in 1976 in the Casavatore area of the city. Three girls, aged 14 to 16, burned to death in a tiny clothing factory in which the exit was blocked by piles of materials. Even after the flames were extinguished, the bodies of the young workers could not be removed, since the water used to douse the fire had flooded the cramped, windowless basement shop; skin divers had to be brought in to do the job.[16]

Child workers in the leather industry have frequently been exposed to dangerous substances such as some adhesives used in footwear production. In the mid-1970s there was a virtual epidemic of respiratory and nervous system diseases among child workers in the south. The glue they had inhaled continued to be used by sweatshop proprietors despite strong public protests. As compensation for this hazardous toil, child workers were being paid the equivalent of $8 to $20 for more than a full week. This form of super-exploitation has become so popular with the small entrepreneurs of the south that if one day all the children of Naples decided not to work, most of the city's industries would collapse immediately.

Another type of precarious labor that arose in the decentralization process was not, like home work and child labor, a return to the past. Instead, it was a practice typical of other industrial countries: the illegal employment of foreigners. Until the early 1970s, Italy was a country which large numbers of people emigrated from, not one they immigrated to. Yet with the great reduction in internal migration from south to north, labor shortages were created in some parts of the country. Many underground businesses resolved the problem by taking on foreigners who lacked work permits. In 1978 the research organization CENSIS estimated the presence of illegal foreign workers at 280,000 to 400,000. A later calculation put the number at 800,000.[17] These immigrants, who are mainly from northern Africa and Yugoslavia, are concentrated in Rome and the large cities of the north. Like their counterparts in the US and other parts of Western Europe, they are usually employed under the worst conditions doing the dirty work that is shunned by the native-born work-force.

The final form of *lavoro nero* that appeared in Italy was off-the-books moonlighting by workers with regular jobs. In this case most of the participants were male and were concentrated in two groups: public workers, whose working day ended at 2 p.m., leaving plenty of time for additional pursuits; and northern industrial workers, whose system of guarantees (including strict limits on overtime and the ability to take days off fairly frequently) facilitated moonlighting even though it was often prohibited in labor contracts.[18]

Although the total working day or work week for regular and secondary occupations combined may have been quite long and comparable to that of home workers, the degree of exploitation of moonlighters was usually much lower. This was because a fair number of them were selling services on their own account or were working for small firms that were willing to pay well and off the books for special skills. In either case the hourly income from moonlighting has tended to be high, and sometimes it even exceeded what was being earned in the regular job.

Moonlighting skilled workers are indeed, as some Italian observers have put it, a kind of aristocracy of precarious labor. It is their situation that people have highlighted when attempting to depict the underground economy as a realm of enhanced living standards and autonomy. Economist Andrea Saba, who has suggested that decentralized production may help bring about a system of true industrial democracy, has said of the 'superior' form of *lavoro nero*:

> The creativity is certainly greater, the alienation less, the social mobility enhanced. Worker participation, even if in atypical forms, is greater; productivity is good; there is a strong development of new technologies . . . and above all there is 'spontaneity'.[19]

Workers in a wide variety of situations have taken advantage of the relatively well-paying and untaxed employment possibilities of the submerged economy. It has been especially common, for instance, among people receiving payment from the *cassa integrazione guadagni*, a type of unemployment program in which a high percentage of one's former wage is paid to workers whose services are no longer needed by their employers but who cannot be legally laid off. The arrangement is supposed to be temporary, but the chronic problems of large Italian corporations have created a class of long-term recipients. While they are barred from doing other paid work while receiving the benefits, the unreported activities of the informal sector have proved an irresistible temptation for many.

Home building is an activity that is widely performed by moonlighters operating off the books. ISTAT data on new residential construction, which are based on housing permits, have fallen far short of the number of new dwellings hooked up with electricity by the state-owned utility ENEL. A study of cumulative statistics from 1972 to 1979 found that ENEL provided electricity to 3.1 million new homes during that period, while ISTAT reported the completion of only 1.5 million dwellings.[20]

There are even people who have been moonlighting in agriculture. Studies of employees of the few large factories of the south, especially the huge Italsider plant in Taranto, have found that many are using their free time to resume their prior occupation as small farmers.[21]

The two underground economies

In looking at the diverse situations of the submerged economy it is clear that that unofficial realm possesses a social and economic hierarchy of its own. Not everyone working off the books falls into the category of wretched sweatshop slave or that of high-living, moonlighting entrepreneur. In Italy, as in other countries, the underground economy is a politically ambiguous phenomenon because it improves the lives of some and worsens that of others.

To some extent, the differentiation of conditions in the Italian underground follows geographical lines. The submerged economy of the northern and central parts of the country is characterized by a fairly high technical level and its participants are to a great degree moonlighting regular workers. Pay and working conditions are relatively good, and the firms that organize the decentralized work are fairly stable enterprises rather than fly-by-night operations. Some of them have achieved a measure of autonomy from the large corporations and sell their products directly to customers, many of whom are abroad. On a national basis, some 35 per cent of Italy's exports have been attributed to small firms.[22]

The underground firms of the south conform more to the conventional pattern of underdevelopment. They are not only small, they are also marginal. That is, they are unstable, under-capitalized, and much more susceptible to sudden changes in market conditions. The production they carry out is much more labor-intensive and less technologically sophisticated. They need the cheapest possible labor and thus often resort to using children. The underground industries of Naples, for instance, are not simply decentralized, they are atomized; more than 10,000 tiny workshops have been estimated to exist in that city alone.

Within the 'advanced' underground economy of the north and center, a key element appears to be a fair degree of political and social stability, including limited worker unrest. It is significant that two of the most dynamic regions of the submerged sector are Veneto and Emilia-Romagna, the first solidly controlled by the Christian Democrats and the second by the Communist Party. The success of the industrial restructuring in these areas can be attributed in part to the political use that these two major parties have made of the process.

In the case of the Christian Democrats there has been a clear encouragement of decentralization in order to promote the ideology of 'traditional' capitalism (owner-operated small enter-prises) and to attack the labor movement. The underground economy thus represented, as one analyst has put it, 'The businessman's vision of the small firm as a place of subdued class conflict . . . It looks to the dismantling of the labor movement in the name of a mythical liberty in individual contract'.[23]

What is surprising is that the attitude of the Italian Communist Party (PCI) in Emilia and elsewhere has not been much different. The PCI has created its own version of the unabashed free enterprise ideology that has been adopted by Italian business, including the attack on the labor movement. Since 1979 at least some factions within the party have wanted to turn their back on the traditional political base of the PCI – the work-force in the key industrial sectors – and criticize both unions and the rank and file for making unreasonable demands. The leading voice in this group (until his death in 1980) was Giorgio Amendola, a 50-year veteran of the party, a hero of the Resistance and a member of the PCI Central Committee. In an article published in the party weekly, *Rinascita*, Amendola charged the labor movement with irresponsibility for allowing worker demands 'to rise uncontrollably' and without commensurate increases in productivity.[24]

This was the same general position that had been espoused by Italian business and the more conservative parties. The PCI's change in direction was part of its attempt to draw political support from the middle class in its persistent but futile quest for a role in the national government. Among these new supporters targeted by the party were the new small businessmen of the underground economy. Starting in the late 1970s the PCI made its pitch to this group through the publication of a slick magazine called *New Orientation for Small and Medium Industry*. Describing itself as a publication for 'democratic entrepreneurs', *New Orientation* editorialized on the need for 'constructing alliances with the strongest sectors of smaller business in order to achieve an economic renewal of the country'.[25]

The PCI has insisted that its gesture to entrepreneurs was not meant to sanction ruthless exploitation of labor. According to one party analysis of the matter, a distinction must be made between those firms engaged in 'wild' decentralization and abuse of workers, and those small firms which restructure in a 'responsible' way in order to achieve higher flexibility and efficiency.[26] Other PCI spokesmen have called the second variety, which they hope will eventually 'emerge' out of the submerged economy and function legally, essential to the future of the country. Whatever one makes of this questionable distinction, it appears that the Communist Party has joined with Italian business in seeing the resolution of that country's economic problems in the permanent weakening of the power of organized labor.

There is little doubt that both forms of the underground economy have contributed to such a weakening. A British observer of the situation has stated that, 'The combination of automation [in the large factories] and decentralization has been specifically aimed at destroying the power and autonomy of the most militant and cohesive section of the Italian proletariat and this strategy has met with considerable success'.[27] The labor movement of the 'hot autumn' ceased to exist by the late 1970s, and even at Fiat, the historic center of militancy, management was able to defeat a major strike and substantially reduce the work-force.

The process of decentralization has, by fragmenting workplaces and (in the case of home labor) isolating workers, put large numbers of people in situations in which it is extremely difficult to organize. In fact, it would be hard to know what kind of organization would be appropriate for precarious workers. An attempt to extend unionization and guarantees to underground firms might serve only to prompt the dissolution of these operations, since their very existence is predicated on the avoidance of labor standards more or less adhered to by regular companies.

The situation is all the more politically sensitive in Italy because the underground economy provides employment, albeit under poor conditions, for groups of workers such as housewives and teenagers who might otherwise be shut out of waged work entirely. For them, as well as for better paid moonlighters, the fact that off-the-books work appears as an individual and often secretive activity means that one is less likely to consider collective political action to improve the conditions under which that labor is performed. The underground realm is thus the economic version of what the Italians call *qualunquismo*, the individualism and self-interest that replaced the political commitment of the late 1960s and early 70s. The adoption of 'bourgeois attitudes' was apparent in an opinion survey that the business magazine *Il Mondo* conducted among employees of decentralized firms of the 'advanced' variety. Most of them expressed satisfaction with their work, confidence in management, and little interest in joining unions.[28]

Striking for the right to evade taxes

As in the US and Britain, the government's approach to dealing with the underground economy in Italy has been ambivalent. Many politicians have accepted the notion of *lavoro nero* as a 'safety valve' that helped to end the upheaval of 1969 and the following years. Yet those responsible for fiscal policy have been concerned about the loss of revenues from business activities that take place off the books. The Finance Ministry has concentrated its efforts on combating the under-reporting of income by individuals and businesses that do not function underground but attempt to evade taxes nonetheless.

In doing this the government went against a long tradition of fiscal non-compliance in Italy. Despite the introduction of the value-added tax in 1973 – which was supposed to make evasion more difficult – small businesses and the self-employed tended to report abnormally low levels of income to the authorities. This was revealed quite clearly when Finance Minister Franco Reviglio issued a series of reports in 1980 as part of a campaign against major tax evaders. By comparing income figures in the national accounts and the declared levels submitted to VAT officials, Reviglio estimated that businesses and the self-employed were reporting only about 50 per cent of their true income, causing the government a loss of VAT revenues of some 9,000 billion lire or about $10 billion. A 1984 revision of the figures put evasion in 1981 at the equivalent of about $18.5 billion.[29]

Reviglio first took aim at restaurants and hotels, which were found to be reporting only about a third of their revenues. The weapon he used was a form called *la ricevuta fiscale* (the fiscal receipt). The government announced that beginning in March 1980 all of the country's 100,000 restaurants and hotels would have to use these receipts for all of their customers. The numbered bills, which were to be available only from state-supervised printers, were supposed to make it easier for tax authorities to determine the true level of revenues for these businesses. Once the law took effect, inspectors were to make spot checks outside restaurants and fine both proprietor and patron when a customer was found leaving without the official bill.

Owners of public establishments fought the law passionately, and in February 1980 Italy experienced its first strike by restaurateurs (hoteliers decided at the last minute not to participate). Three-quarters of the country's bars and nearly all of the eating places supported the one-day action and kept their doors locked. The major exception was Bologna, since restaurant proprietors in that culinary center decided they could not bear to deprive their customers even for one day.

The strike did not succeed in altering the government's plans, though, as expected, shrewd Italian businessmen found a way around the law. They simply made use of a lively black market in forged fiscal receipts. But the battle continued. In 1983 the Finance Ministry targeted all retail businesses with a law requiring them to use tamper-proof electronic cash registers with sealed memory banks. Yet this technique, too, was far from foolproof in thwarting determined tax evaders. All the proprietor had to do was ring up a price lower than that actually received.[30]

The tenacity of the Italian shopkeeper in trying to hide much of his or her income from the government symbolizes the passion with which the country engages in underground activity.

There has been a growing sense in Italy that regular and legitimate economic pursuits are not the best financial route to security. The basic economic structure remains somewhat shaky, and it is only by people operating informally in and around institutions that things somehow stay together.

To some extent, l'economia sommersa is a typically Italian ambiguous solution to an intractable situation. But it is also an arrangement that has come into being in a wide variety of countries throughout the world. In most cases the movement of productive activity underground results from a serious but not fatal weakness of the regular economy. In response to this condition, business seeks to restructure production to increase profitability, and individuals seek new forms of income-earning activity in order to maintain a decent standard of living. The more or less stable equilibrium that results is the 'Italian solution'.

8. Development and under(ground)development

Much of the discussion of the underground economy and the broader social transformation in the developed countries revolves around the notion of dualism. The idea is that the restructuring of the economy is bringing with it a deterioriation of working and living conditions for a significant part of the population. Instead of the 1950s model of an increasingly 'affluent society', the new prediction is for more people to fall into a second-class existence of poorly-paying and unstable jobs and general economic insecurity. What were previously conditions faced mainly by the ghetto population are becoming the norm for growing numbers of others.

Aside from the ghetto, the precedent for the tendency toward dualism was the third world. After the Second World War, the spread of US, European and Japanese business across the globe brought about situations in which modern production facilities sprang up next to smaller-scale and less sophisticated operations. The dynamics of development in Asia, Africa and Latin America came to be put in terms of the relationship between what were called the modern and the traditional sectors. The development orthodoxy pushed by the World Bank and other international agencies in the 1950s and 1960s was to shrink the traditional sector and build the modern one through the expansion of production for export in the world market.

By the 1970s it became clear that this approach was not succeeding in lifting most third world countries out of a position of subordination and poverty. Transnational corporations were still investing in the less developed countries, but the capital that was flowing in was doing a lot more for the profit statements of those companies than for the development status of the 'host' nations. The increasing mobility of capital and the general world economic crisis limited the bargaining power of third world countries and set back their hopes of economic independence. Small numbers of workers found jobs in the modern sector, while most of the labor force in third world countries remained unemployed, under-employed or trapped in marginal activities.

This state of affairs caused some economists in the west to begin turning the prevailing development paradigm on its head. The traditional sector was suddenly no longer viewed as a brake on development but rather as an important resource for third world economies. Small and 'backward' enterprises were no longer denounced as inefficient users of resources and employers of excess numbers of low-productivity workers. 'Primitive' technology became 'appropriate technology'; small was now beautiful. To go along with this revolution in thinking there was a shift in terminology: the traditional economy was now the informal sector.

The catalyst for this change in theory has been widely seen in the work of anthropologist Keith Hart. In a paper delivered in 1971, Hart declared that informal production 'offers itself as a means of salvation . . . Denied success by the formal opportunity structure, these members of the urban sub-proletariat seek informal means of increasing their incomes'.[1] Basing his conclusions on research carried out in parts of Ghana, Hart created a taxonomy of 'income opportunities' ranging from regular jobs in private companies or the government to illegitimate activities such as drug-pushing, prostitution, smuggling and protection rackets. In between were informal activities related to small-scale production of goods and services and distribution. For Hart the main distinction between formal and informal activities was that the latter involved self-employment. In this way even the beggar eking out the most miserable income was viewed as an example of 'indigenous enterprise'.

Hart's article was refreshing in its unprejudiced view of the spectrum of human activities, yet he was not critical enough in his use of self-employment as the distinguishing characteristic of informal work. He did not take into account that many forms of self-employment are far from autonomous, and he thus laid the groundwork for an apologetic view of underdevelopment. This is precisely what emerged in a 1972 report by the International Labour Office (ILO) on the problems of economic growth in

Kenya. The authors of the study boldly presented the informal sector as a key part of a strategy for increasing employment in that country:

> For observers surrounded by imported steel, glass and concrete, it requires a leap of the imagination and considerable openness of mind to perceive the informal sector as a sector of thriving economic activity and a source of Kenya's future wealth.[2]

They insisted that such a change of perspective was justified, and they called on both international agencies and the Kenyan government to adopt policies that encouraged rather than hampered the expansion of the informal sector. After estimating that in 1969 up to 33 per cent of urban employment in Kenya was in that sector, the ILO analysts got to the heart of the matter by stating: 'For many individuals and their families, and urban women, the informal sector may provide the only income opportunity that is available.'[3]

In the wake of the Kenya report, there was a veritable explosion of studies of the informal sector throughout the third world. Much of the research was sponsored by the ILO, and the general consensus was that the promotion of informal activities was indeed the main hope for many underdeveloped countries. Almost overnight, this call won the support of a significant portion of the 'development establishment'.

It was not much longer before a group of critics arose in opposition and pointed out the dark side of informal production. The Kenya report was taken to task for concentrating on what characterized an informal firm and saying little about what conditions were faced by a worker in the sector. S.V. Sethuraman summarized these conditions as being *unprotected* (without union and government guarantees), *unenumerated* (not counted in official statistics), and *underemployed* (paid very low wages and working irregularly).[4] Other characteristics which emerged from empirical work included: variability in the hours of labor, erratic income levels, limited job security, and low levels of skill in a conventional sense. Ray Bromley and Chris Gerry termed this kind of employment *casual work* and offered the simple definition:

'any way of making a living which lacks a moderate degree of security of income and employment'.[5]

The critics also raised questions about the autonomy of firms and individuals in the informal sector. The Kenya study and Hart (though in different ways) had encouraged analysts to view participants in the sector as entrepreneurs of a sort. Acting outside the institutions of society, these industrious individuals were supposedly doing well for themselves despite the economic problems of the country as a whole.

It is undeniable that many informal sector participants do not toil under customary wage relationships and that their income levels are related to the amount of effort they put into their productive activities. Yet the absence of a wage relationship does not necessarily make one into a businessman in any meaningful sense. This is seen in some of the truly marginal activities that have been examined in the research on casual work. Chris Birkbeck, for instance, studied the scavengers in the garbage dumps of Cali, Colombia:

> The garbage picker may work hard, may have a shrewd eye for saleable materials, may search long for the right buyer; in short, he may be the near-perfect example of the enterprising individual. It will not get him far.[6]

Aside from being reduced to a miserable sort of work, the garbage pickers of Cali also turned out to be highly dependent on the formal sector; their autonomy was quite dubious. Bromley and Gerry decided that the conditions of the informal sector actually consisted of a continuum including short-term wage work, disguised wage work, dependent work, and true self-employment.[7]

The question of autonomy also turns on what one takes to be the basic relationship between the informal and formal sectors. The Kenya report suggested that there should be prosperous co-existence of the two, which were seen as essentially separate from one another. Policymakers could easily choose to promote the informal sector and this was seen as relieving the plight of the unemployed.

This 'innocent' approach conveniently ignores the role played by the informal sector on behalf of regular enterprises owned both by third world entrepreneurs and transnational corporations. Alejandro Portes and John Walton, for instance, have argued that the informal sector provides essential goods and services at a cheap enough level so that the employers of workers in formal businesses can keep wages at an absolute minimum. In this way, the informal sector is subsidizing the formal one.[8]

Subcontracting to the underground

There is evidence that the informal sector is even more directly integrated into the new international division of labor. Classical Marxism would suggest that the displaced peasants who join the informal sector in the cities constitute a reserve army of labor for regular capitalist enterprises. This is certainly true to some extent. But what is new about the informal sector that has arisen in the third world since the beginning of the 1970s is that multinational and local firms have been able to make use of labor from that sector instead of hiring workers directly into regular enterprises. What brought this about was the rise of international subcontracting.

Until the late 1960s, the predominant form of multinational corporate expansion was direct investment. Subsidiaries of giant firms were established in third world countries to manufacture products that were sold either in the local market or abroad. Seeking to avoid the political problems and occasional expropriations that resulted from these investments, transnationals started using a new approach. They split up the production process and subcontracted out the various phases to factories located around the world. The semi-finished components were brought together in the firm's home country or some other central location for final assembly.

US-based corporations pioneered this practice with the establishment of the border industrialization program with Mexico in 1965. Since then subcontracting, especially in the electronics industry, has grown rapidly. The value of subcontracted components brought back to the US for final assembly and distribution rose from less than $1 billion in 1966 to $18 billion in 1982.[9] Some of the future growth is likely to come from the subcontracting of clerical rather than industrial work. Through the use of satellites, companies have begun to have more of their data-entry work done in third world countries. Barbados seems to be the favored place thus far for these 'offshore offices'.[10]

Whether the subcontractors were subsidiaries of the larger firm (as in Ford's global sourcing arrangement for producing automobiles) or formally autonomous, the arrangement had numerous advantages for the transnational corporation. It allowed a much greater degree of flexibility in output and a great reduction in risk, since the corporation was not exposing fully integrated production facilities to the vagaries of foreign politics. If the subcontractor was independent, there was no risk at all, since the capital was being invested by someone else. And the subcontractor was also left with the dirty work of managing underpaid and overworked employees. An OECD report also candidly discussed how the practice helped to weaken the power of the transnational's employees at home:

> Sub-contracting may provide a solution to work slowdowns or stoppages due to labour negotiations or strikes. In Europe over the past few years, there has been a tendency – although it is still rather hesitant – for workers to demonstrate their international solidarity at the prompting of multinational trade unions. If this trend gathers strength, it should become increasingly difficult to switch sub-contracting relations within the same region. This is why it is necessary to extend the network of sub-contracting relations further afield and to increase the number of agreements with firms in the developing countries that are beyond the reach of workers' organizations.[11]

This restructuring of international manufacturing is analogous to the process of productive decentralization which developed in Italy during the same period. In both cases larger facilities were broken down into geographically dispersed operations which provided much greater flexibility for management but made it much more difficult for workers to organize.

While some of the subcontracting factories of the third world remained in the formal sector in those countries, there has been some additional dispersal into the informal sector. Production is often farmed out further to tiny workshops and home work enterprises that operate unofficially. This is seen, for instance, in the garment industry of the Philippines. The majority of the 500,000 workers involved in that industry are employed by tiny subcontractors to perform their work in small shops or at home on a piecework basis. One writer who interviewed rural home workers in the province of Bulacan found the women earning about 600 centavos (equivalent to about 72 cents) a day.[12]

The dispersed workers were used both as a source of cheap labor and as a tool for undermining struggles by employees of regular factories. In 1977 a group of clothing workers at the firm of Greenfield & Santiago in Manila secretly formed a union. When management learned of this they suspended all of the workers who had supported the union and shifted a good deal of production over to home workers. Although the act was a blatant violation of local labor law, the Philippine government did everything to support the employer.[13]

In this way, Manila was following the pattern of many third world governments in pursuing policies that, aside from undermining unions, end up promoting the informal sector. The Brazilian government, for instance, has been assisting what are called microbusinesses (about half of which are based in the homes of the owners) by essentially permitting them to operate off the books. The discovery of the extent of these tiny entrepreneurial operations has given a different reputation to the notorious slums of Brazil's cities. One academic observer has declared: 'Some people say, go into a "*favela*" and you'll emerge a communist, but I think the opposite is true. I go in and I come out marveling at private initiative.'[14]

That private initiative can take a variety of forms in the third world. In some cases it consists more of criminal enterprise and tax evasion than small-scale production. The following sections look at two countries where the former sorts of underground economy have reached remarkable proportions.

The underground Wild West of Colombia

The informal sector of Colombia is an underground economy based predominantly on smuggling, and the main contraband is illicit drugs.[15] During the past decade Colombia has become one of the world's leading suppliers of marijuana and cocaine, especially for the US market. The enormous profits available in the drug business have made it one of the largest components of the country's economy.

Colombian economists have estimated the drug trade at about $3 billion a year. About half of the 'narcodollars' are thought to be held abroad, but the substantial remainder fuels a thriving *otra economía* of black market dollars circulating in Colombia or converted into pesos. The flow of dollars into the country has been so huge that Colombia is the only place in the world where the black market exchange rate for dollars has been *lower* than the official one. The government of Colombia enjoys phenomenal foreign reserve levels as a result of this trend, especially since it set up *la ventanilla siniestra* at the national bank in 1976. This 'left-handed window' has allowed people to convert black market dollars into 'clean' pesos. Yet the government has also been concerned about the negative impact that the flood of narcotics money has on the economy.

In 1979 the Colombian ambassador to the US, Diego Ascencio, testified before a Senate hearing on illegal narcotics profits, declaring that the drug trade had a variety of 'corrosive effects' on the economic and social structures of his country.[16] Ascencio noted that income from the drug trade was estimated to have risen to a level equivalent to nearly 20 per cent of the country's money supply. This brought about a rapid increase in inflation, especially in real estate and construction. The central bank sought to contain the price rises by tightening credit, but this had the effect of squeezing out all but the biggest corporations. Smaller borrowers had to resort to the parallel credit market that was funded by drug money and which charged substantially higher interest rates. The combination of higher prices and restricted credit, according to Ascencio, had a devastating effect. Other analysts have agreed and have noted that the lion's share of the drug income goes to only a few hundred people. The small marijuana farmer gets only about seven per cent of the crop's export value. Waged workers of marijuana-growing and cocaine-processing facilities (the coca leaf originates in Peru and Bolivia and is turned into cocaine hydrochloride in Colombia) are paid more than employees of the average legal enterprise, but they are hardly becoming rich.

The average Colombian is affected by the drug trade in roughly the same way in which workers in other third world countries are affected by international subcontracting. Instead of working directly for foreign capital, they are employed by domestic suppliers who enjoy astronomical rates of profit. But whereas the political climate engendered by export-oriented production in other countries has often been repressive, the situation in Colombia has been more anarchic. Narcotics entrepreneurs have corrupted many of the country's politicians to ensure relatively unimpeded commerce, which often includes bloody disputes between different operations. The level of violence in the country has reached an alarming level, causing one observer to describe the areas of drug trafficking as 'little Dodge Cities without the good marshal'.[17] Here it is not a matter of the state promoting or combating the informal economy (though some measures of the latter sort have been attempted); it is an underground realm of the criminal variety that has taken over large parts of the country.

'Black money' in India

The substantial volume of underground income in India stems only to a limited extent from outright criminal activities.[18] The main sources instead are the pervasive black market and the widespread under-reporting of revenues from legitimate business pursuits. The black market has been a problem in India for decades. Profiteers have repeatedly cornered the market for various agricultural and manufactured commodities, despite government measures both before and after independence. As a result, prices for many essential products have risen rapidly over the years, contributing to the economic misery of a large part of the population.

The accumulation of unreported income is not limited to entrepreneurs functioning exclusively in the black market. The private sector in India – both small and large businesses – is notorious for hiding the true volume of its activities from the state. Many transactions are conducted with two components: that valued in 'clean' money that will be reported to the authorities, and a supplementary amount that will be kept off the books. The combination of under-reported regular income and black market profits has reached so high a level that the London *Economist* has declared that India 'is awash with "black money" '.[19]

The attempts to measure the volume of unofficial income and the taxes evaded on it have a long history. The economist Nicholas Kaldor anticipated the analyses of the 1970s in the US and the UK with a 1956 report on the Indian tax system. By comparing the national accounts to the income reported on tax returns, Kaldor estimated unreported income in the 1955–6 financial year at 200–300 crores (a crore equals 10 million rupees) or about two per cent of the GDP. The informal government estimate at the time was only about a tenth as much.

The Kaldor method became the basis for a series of subsequent estimates by Indian government bodies. The Wanchoo Committee put underground income at 1400 crores (four per cent of GDP) in 1968–9 and estimates in the late 1970s were as high as 7,000 crores (more than eight per cent). Later journalistic accounts have put the figure at 20 per cent or more of the official economy.[20]

The Indian government has attempted a variety of measures through the years to combat tax evasion and bring accumulated underground money back into the realm of legitimacy. Back in 1946 there was the first of the indirect coercive measures. Long before James Henry proposed it and the IRS considered it for the US, India carried out a recall of large denomination currency. This process of demonetization was repeated in 1978, but in both instances the impact was not enormous. In the absence of rigorous tax enforcement, much of the unreported income was being held in bank accounts, thus making it immune from the recall scheme. In addition, the extent of hidden income was pervasive enough so that an attack on big bills was inadequate; people went on hoarding and circulating rupees in smaller denominations.

From 1951 to 1975 the government also attempted a number of voluntary disclosure schemes. Tax evaders were guaranteed freedom from prosecution if they came forward and declared their hidden income and paid taxes on it. These measures were a bit more successful, recovering a cumulative total of roughly 500 crores in tax revenues on 2,500 crores of income.

Yet the amount of income that remained hidden was estimated

to be at least equal to the amount that was disclosed. To bring to light yet more of the underground economy the government adopted a novel and controversial plan in 1981. Tax evaders were allowed to purchase a special bearer bond offered by the government. These bonds had a face value of 10,000 rupees and paid 20 per cent interest over a maturity of 10 years. In other words, the government was not only providing amnesty to evaders but was also eliminating taxes on the unreported income that went into the purchase of the bonds and paying interest on the investment to boot. Naturally, the plan was roundly denounced by some members of parliament who regarded it as immoral and as a violation of the government's responsibility to enforce the tax laws. A more tolerant Indian economist considered the financial difficulties of his government and decided the scheme was 'essentially a public borrowing out of black monetary resources at a relatively low rate of interest'.[21]

The comparatively soft stance that the Indian government has taken toward tax evaders may be related to the fact that a number of politicians have been tainted by 'black money'. As in Colombia, the huge amount of extra cash available to major underground operators has allowed them to shower improper and outright illegal payments on political candidates and government officials. The use of 'black money' for political contributions accelerated after the banning of direct donations by business in 1969. During the 1977 national election, according to the *Far Eastern Economic Review*, Indira Gandhi's Congress Party received 160 million rupees (then about $23 million) in contributions from business in the form of advertisements in souvenir booklets that were never printed.[22] Those funds, along with a much smaller amount received by the opposing Janata Party in similarly dubious ways, largely came from slush funds of 'black money' set aside by businesses. The Janata Party, which won that election, did enact some harsh penalties for black marketeers, but there was no evidence that this did much to inhibit the functioning of the underground economy.

The end of the third world?

The underground economies of Colombia and India seem to have more in common with off-the-books activities in the US and

Western Europe than with informal production in other parts of the third world.[23] Yet the comparisons are not so straightforward. The drug trade of Colombia is, like the garment industry of the Philippines for instance, highly integrated into an international system of production and distribution. In the latter case, the system is dominated by 'legitimate' transnational corporations that operate with the blessings of government; in the former, the international commerce is conducted by mafia-type organizations that violate the law but often have unofficial links with politicians, intelligence agencies, etc. In each example there is a complicated combination of elements that are 'modern' (global integration, mass production) and those that are 'traditional' (labor-intensive work, home-based production).

The Indian underground economy shares with analogous activities in the advanced countries a preoccupation with tax evasion. Whereas for most third world countries the attempt to quantify the informal sector through estimating fiscal cheating was barely considered by analysts of the subject, in India the measurement debate actually began long before it became popular in the US and Europe. Yet the central role played by black marketeering gives India's informal economy the look of under-development. The ability of profiteers to easily manipulate supply and demand for certain essential commodities is a reminder of how shaky the overall economy of the country remains.

All of this is to say that there is no clear relationship between the underground economy and the stage of development of a country. The existence of a large volume of unreported and unmeasured economic activity may be indicative of either a low or high stage of socio-economic evolution. This is particularly the case where informal production gets mixed in with the international capitalist division of labor. The combination of global integration and social transformation in the developed countries makes it increasingly difficult to distinguish the third world from the first one. Many of the characteristics of the informal sector in Asia, Africa and Latin America – whether marginal production, subcontracting, dope trafficking or tax evasion – are just as applicable to North America and Western Europe.

Ironically, the underground economy in a sense achieves something above-ground development failed to accomplish:

bridging the gap between developed and underdeveloped countries. Unfortunately, this is taking place not by bringing the third world up to the standards of living in the advanced countries, but rather by pulling the first world down and making precarious labor and economic insecurity a more universal state of affairs. It may be that in the third world, as in the first, there are some people who are able to use informal activity to achieve a better economic existence, but they are a distinct minority.

9. The second economy in the Soviet bloc

The mythology of Soviet 'socialism' has historically relied on the depiction of a population willing to toil energetically at the service of the state. During Lenin's time unpaid work on Saturday (the *subbotnik*) was promoted, and in the Stalin era the Stakhanovite super-worker was widely celebrated. Workers were expected to exert themselves for the cause of building socialism, and anyone who refused stood in danger of being branded a social parasite.

The people of the Soviet Union are indeed industrious, but over time more and more of their activity has come to be directed at personal rather than collective gain. Within the centralized and socialized economy, there began to proliferate small-scale (and sometimes not so small) transactions that escaped the planning process. By the 1970s Soviet experts in the west and emigré scholars were talking of a *second economy* in the Soviet Union.[1] A former Moscow correspondent of the *New York Times* put it well:

> Corruption and illegal private enterprise in Russia, 'creeping capitalism', as some Russians playfully call it, grow out of the very nature of the Soviet economy and its inefficiencies – shortages, poor quality goods, terrible delays in service. They constitute more than a black market as westerners are accustomed to thinking of it. For parallel to the official economy, there exists an entire, thriving counter-economy . . . [which] has become an integral part of the Soviet system, a built-in, permanent feature of Soviet society.[2]

It is only the most die-hard apologists for the Soviet Union who can deny that the economy of that country has not been terribly successful in meeting the material needs of the population. While the kind of utter destitution that exists in parts of the third world and west may not exist, the people of the Soviet Union and Eastern Europe have had to live with inadequate supplies of many goods and inferior quality for those that are available. To some extent then, participation in the second economy has simply been a matter of survival, of seeking to maintain a decent standard of living in a system that did not always 'deliver the goods'. Yet the upper reaches of the illegal private sector do include some full-blown, western-style business.

Living 'on the left'

Some analysts of the subject place the origins of the second economy in the late 1950s, when the Soviet government, seeking to increase its hard currency reserves, first began promoting foreign tourism. Yet the state's expected windfall of dollars and Deutsch-marks never materialized. It turned out that the black market in foreign currency expanded substantially as western visitors changed their money on the street rather than in banks.[3] This infusion of hard cash stimulated the smuggling of goods from abroad, and the black market grew by leaps and bounds. It reached such a point in the early 1960s that the government had to take drastic action. In 1961 the death penalty for serious economic crimes was reinstituted (it was previously in existence from 1932 to 1947), and two major currency speculators were promptly executed.

There is no evidence that such draconian punishment seriously inhibited the development of the second economy. While the big-time operators had to be careful – and distribute their bribes generously – the magnitude of the everyday hustling that developed among the population made it difficult for the authorities to crack down. It was rapidly becoming a way of life for people to get the goods and services they needed 'on the side', or in the wonderfully ironic Russian phrase, *na levo* (literally, 'on the left').

The variety of unofficial economic activities in the Soviet Union is so great that analysts have described a virtual spectrum of 'colored markets'. One Soviet expert has proposed the following scheme:

Legal markets	'red' –	state-owned and operated enterprises;
	'pink' –	state shops through which people buy and sell used goods;
	'white' –	flea markets for used durable goods; small concessions for the sale of fruits and vegetables.
Semi-legal markets	'gray' –	unofficial and informal sales of goods and services, such as private tutoring; also informal exchanges of materials among state factory managers.
Illegal markets	'brown' –	irregular transactions through state shops; trade in goods brought back by people traveling abroad;
	'black' –	speculation in legal commodities, semi-legal commodities (foreign goods) and illegal commodities (gold, foreign currency, narcotics); criminal activities (prostitution).[4]

This scheme does not state exactly where the second economy begins and is thus useful for description but not analysis. The distinction between the private and the public sectors is also not sufficient. Although the Soviet Union has been much less liberal in this regard than the countries of Eastern Europe, there has been some legalization of private transactions (the 'white' category above); yet it is common for legalized trade to be expanded far beyond what the state planners had intended when they lifted the prohibition. Perhaps most common is the growth of home production of fruits and vegetables into an extensive business. Farmers, especially from areas such as Georgia, are famous for loading suitcases full of tomatoes, grapes, flowers and other high-priced items and flying long distances to Moscow. There they sell the merchandise at a substantial profit, even taking into account the transportation costs.

The traveling greengrocer and florist have become such familiar figures in the Soviet Union that there are popular jokes about them. Hedrick Smith recounts a tale about a flight from Tbilisi to Moscow that someone tried to hijack to the west. A Georgian man overpowered the hijacker and allowed the plane to reach its intended destination. As he was being decorated for his supposed heroism, the man was asked by a government official what induced him to act. He responded, 'What was I going to do with 5,000 carnations in Paris?'[5]

In place of the legal/illegal and public/private distinctions, some analysts have suggested defining the second economy as the realm of activities that are not figured into the country's official plan (legal private transactions are included). This seems a reasonable enough working definition, and it also has the advantage of suggesting the analogy with underground economic activity in the west. In both cases those transactions that are 'other' are those that occur without the knowledge and control or supervision of the state.

Whereas in the west the point of going underground is to increase one's disposable income (or in the case of an informal employer, to cut costs by evading taxes and paying substandard wages), the Soviet second economy is first and foremost concerned with the problem of supply. It provides goods and services that are otherwise not available at all, available but of poor quality, or available only after long periods of waiting. Cost is not central here; in fact, the prices of commodities in the second economy are invariably much higher than those obtained through official channels. This is true in comparison to what is on sale in both regular shops and the special outlets accessible only to higher-level government and party officials. In the latter case, the goods are of superior quality (and often of western make) but artificially cheap in price.

From *blat* to underground capitalism

It is extremely difficult to estimate the size of the second economy in the Soviet Union. The techniques used in the west to measure the underground economy simply do not work. The method relating to currency in circulation cannot be used, since the Soviet government has since the 1930s treated monetary data as a state secret. Measuring a potential underground labor force is hampered by the fact that everyone must have an official occupation, so everyone who is not a student, a housewife, a pensioner or an invalid is counted as employed. Using this classification, the second economy is primarily one of moonlighters.

Despite these obstacles, Andrei Sakharov has been quoted as estimating the second economy at about 10 per cent of the official one, but he apparently based that figure on nothing more than impressions.[6] More promising is the work being conducted among Soviet emigrés in Israel. Interviews with groups of recent arrivals have determined that families had earned an average of 12 per cent of their income and had made an average of 18 per cent of their expenditures in the second economy,[7] though the experience of these emigrés may not be typical.

What complicates both definitional and quantitative efforts is that the second economy exists in the midst of the official one. At the simplest and perhaps most innocent level, the second economy involves what is known in Russian as *blat*, i.e. the use of influence and connections to get things done in a highly bureaucratic society. Sometimes this is merely a matter of exchanging favors, and in that sense is not, strictly speaking, within the realm of economics. Yet *blat* often develops into *vzyatka*, the petty bribery that is frequently necessary to get employees of state businesses to make available goods and services that would otherwise require long periods of waiting. This extends from forms of tipping to elaborate arrangements in which state goods are diverted and sold entirely for private profit.

These kinds of activity, comparable to what in Britain are called 'fiddles', can be divided into several major categories:

- paying and receiving bribes related to the performance of a regular job;
- selling state property for private gain (one of the most common forms of this is the sale of state gasoline by official chauffeurs[8]);
- appropriating state materials for personal use;
- converting state resources into a private enterprise (such as the state auto repair shops where customers wanting

faster and better service make private deals with the mechanics).

Konstantin Simis, a former criminal lawyer in the Soviet Union now living in the west, argued in his book on Soviet corruption that in light of low salary levels, such supplementary forms of income-earning are essential for the average Soviet family if it is to maintain even a subsistence level of consumption.[9]

The means of survival and, for some, of living comfortably, are also obtained in ways that are not so strictly job-related. A wide array of services such as private tutoring, dressmaking, babysitting, and household repair are, practically speaking, available only in the second economy. Home building would probably not be possible without the *shabashniki*, the groups of freelance workers who sell their services on an unofficial basis. Some of these are moonlighters from regular jobs and others risk doing this contract work on a full-time basis.

Unofficial transactions in goods and currency correspond more closely to what westerners think of as the black market. But there are actually a few different types of activity involved. First, there is the familiar illicit changing of money and trading of goods such as blue jeans and records. The arrival of smuggled video-cassette players into some Russian households has made videotapes a rapidly growing part of this sector.[10] The black market often blends into the more directly criminal world. Although Soviet authorities are loath to admit it, crime has not disappeared in post-capitalist society. A number of colorful accounts have been published in the west of a thriving Soviet underworld.[11]

What is more surprising is the evidence that has come to light in recent years that fairly sizeable underground productive enterprises have functioned, despite the strict laws against them and the rigorous enforcement by the OBKhSS, the state agency charged with combating speculation and theft of socialist property. On-the-job fiddles and moonlighting generally involves the provision of private services or circumvention of the usual problems of distribution of state-produced merchandise. What was thought to be impossible to carry out in the Soviet Union was unofficial *manufacturing of goods*. Yet it turned out that while the risks and obstacles were substantial, it was possible to create a capitalist-type business under the nose of the 'socialist' state.

The simplest form of this is the widespread practice of producing moonshine vodka for personal consumption and limited sale. One western expert claimed that more than 250,000 people were involved in making home-brewed alcohol.[12] Reports have also surfaced of small businesses engaged in other sorts of light industry.[13] At times this has been based on a classic capitalist form of production that has been reappearing in many countries with the growth of the underground economy: home labor. Unofficial producers of blue jeans, for instance, have made use of home workers to manufacture the garments, which are then sold in the black market along with imported versions. In other cases, the entrepreneurs of the second economy set up secret facilities outside workers' homes. Sometimes these are based within state-owned factories, with plant managers using state resources to produce goods that will be sold privately; one expert called this 'private production with an official facade'. It is on-the-job fiddling taken to a much higher level.

The challenges involved in establishing a secret manufacturing operation from scratch in the Soviet Union are formidable. All of the inputs – land, plant, raw materials, labor – must be obtained surreptitiously and there is the constant threat of detection by the OBKhSS. Simis claims that nonetheless, 'a network of private factories is spread across the whole country; these factories manufacture goods to the value of many hundreds of millions – perhaps even billions – of rubles'.[14] He acknowledges that this private industry cannot produce machinery or automobiles but says it can compete with the state in the manufacture of lighter items such as clothing.

Simis tells the story of the Silberg brothers (not their real name), who he says headed a company that owned at least ten factories manufacturing artificial leather goods and synthetic fiber products. Their case demonstrated what is perhaps the secret to (and the pitfall of) underground capitalism in the Soviet Union. According to Simis, the Silbergs' operation was well known to the OBKhSS but prosecution was waived in appreciation of the thousands of rubles in bribes the brothers paid out every month. Things were going smoothly until a lower level OBKhSS officer, perhaps disappointed with his share of the loot, leaked the story to a journalist from *Isvestia*. Extravagant payoffs by the Silbergs prevented their complete demise, but one of the brothers was sent to a prison camp and several of the family's factories were confiscated.[15]

Entrepreneurial socialism in Hungary

Second economies of a similar sort may be found throughout Eastern Europe. One of the most vigorous is that in Hungary. Even the party newspaper *Nepszabadsag* has acknowledged that at least 70 per cent of the country's families receive some part of their income from the second economy.[16] A reporter from the *Wall Street Journal* got a government economist to go even further: '100 per cent might be closer. I don't know anyone who doesn't earn on the side'. The same correspondent quoted a social scientist at Karl Marx University in Budapest as estimating that the second economy provided one-third of the country's production and 40 per cent of personal income in 1981.[17]

István Kemény has argued that the role of unofficial activity has reached a point such that the official figures on incomes are hardly relevant:

> Almost everyone lives *partly*, or – even more exactly – to a *very small extent* from his formal wage or salary. To a far greater extent they live from other activities; from those activities associated with the secondary, parallel, hidden or, more simply, market economy.[18]

In a tongue-in-cheek account of building a house in Hungary, János Kenedi described the unusual methods one has to employ in order to get such a job done. Virtually all the necessary materials were available, but only through complicated irregular arrangements or by flagging down delivery vans on the road and bribing the drivers to divert some of their load. Kenedi claimed that many of the apparent shortages of goods in state shops were actually reflections of arrangements by employees seeking side payments:

> There is no need for dejection and retreat . . . Once your
> hearing is refined enough to understand that the reply: 'We
> haven't got it', really means 'It's under the counter', you will
> never be overwhelmed by hopelessness.[19]

The Hungarian government has taken a fairly tolerant attitude
toward the sort of unofficial economic activity that could easily
land one in jail in the Soviet Union. The general approach has been
to view the second economy as closely linked to legitimate private
enterprise. Rather than cracking down on those businesses that
lacked explicit sanction from the state, the policy has been to try to
get underground entrepreneurs to function legally. It has done
this, above all, by greatly liberalizing the conditions under which
private small business may function in the country.[20] What started
as an attempt to make services available to people outside the
major cities ended up as part of a general encouragement of
relatively free enterprise. This policy, which forms part of what
western accounts have dubbed 'goulash communism', assumes
that a substantial degree of private ownership and management is
essential for the efficient functioning of smaller-scale industry,
retail trade, service businesses, and parts of agriculture.

Western accounts have lavished praise on the signs of Hungary's
relatively high standard of living, which they attribute to the
degree of private enterprise. One observer has noted:

> Privatization and the possibilities for the accumulation of
> private wealth have created a very visible class of truly
> *nouveaux riches* . . . Houses built on three levels, with
> swimming pools and garages to house the BMW's or
> Mercedeses, costing more than $200,000 . . . speak clearly on
> the new wealth of those who have been able to take
> advantage of privatization, of 'entrepreneurial socialism' and
> the second economy.[21]

But the same writer diverges from the purely celebratory accounts
and notes that this new wealth is not accruing to everyone.
Resembling what has been happening in the west, the rise of an
entrepreneurial class has been accompanied by an impoverishment
of another part of the population. In this case it is those

Hungarians who do not have access to lucrative unofficial activities. The government was embarrassed when an independent organization called SZETA (an acronym for Foundation to Support the Poor) was established to help the needy.

The black market and martial law in Poland

In Poland the second economy is more closely related to poverty than to prosperous entrepreneurship. There have been some industrious people, such as unofficial home builders and private suppliers of high-priced flowers and vegetables (known as *badylarze*, or 'weed growers') who maintain large hot-houses outside urban areas.[22] Yet for most Poles the second economy has mainly been a source for scarce goods and a way of hustling vital extra income. Resorting to the black market became essential for survival in the economic climate that developed after the rise of Solidarity and even more so during martial law. The steady decline in the value of the *zloty* generated a pervasive black market for foreign currencies, especially the dollar. Facing severe financial pressure, the Jaruzelski regime sought to exploit this market. The government froze all hard currency assets in state banks and only paid out those funds in *bony*, coupons that were denominated in dollars and could be used to purchase otherwise unavailable goods in the Pewex hard-currency shops. The *bony*, which had previously been used only to give change when someone made a purchase at a Pewex store, started circulating widely as a substitute hard currency (they could be legally traded, whereas dollars and other western money could not).[23]

While seeking to prop up the *zloty* through this unorthodox method, the Jaruzelski regime did take some harsh action against individual participants in the black market. Since 1982 thousands of Poles have been fined or arrested for offenses such as ration-card fraud and hoarding goods for private sale. Yet Stewart Steven wrote in his book on Poland that the government is widely suspected of exploiting the black market. In one sense this is obvious: the second economy siphons off excess purchasing power (brought about by official shortages) and takes some pressure off the government to provide the population with all the goods they need. But Steven went further. He suggested that the government has actually been selling goods through the black market that should have been available in regular shops. He even found something good about this alleged practice:

> It is, when one comes to think of it, a quite brilliant way of raising prices without actually raising prices – of making those who can afford to pay, pay through the nose and subsidize those who cannot.[24]

What this statement fails to point out, of course, is that the channeling of goods through the black market means that they are not available through the official outlets at the subsidized prices. If the practice was indeed taking place, there was nothing enlightened about it; it was simply a cynical way of improving the finances of the state at the expense of the population.

In all, the second economy in the Soviet bloc is partly an outgrowth of corruption and partly a way for people to survive the inability of 'real socialism' to provide an adequate standard of living through regular means. The essential role of the second economy throughout the Soviet bloc suggests that it is not a separate and deviant realm. It is very much part of the system. One can almost conclude that low official wage levels and poor distribution are made possible by the existence of a relatively efficient second economy. By permanently filling in the gaps left by the regular economic institutions, the second economy becomes an institution itself and probably even serves as a political stabilizer. Rather than being a subversive force, it may be the thing that keeps the 'socialist' system from collapsing.

10. Concluding notes from the underground

It is an old but worthy tenet of radical thought that the creation and maintenance of capitalism requires a mass of people to be separated from the land and compelled to sell their labor in order to survive. As a consequence, these 'propertyless workers' are periodically subjected to unemployment, privation and other material difficulties as the erratic economy goes through its fluctuations. The history of the labor movement has basically been an effort to free people from this precarious existence through union organizing and agitation for progressive government policies. The development of the welfare state in this century created a body of protections and guarantees that replaced the tyranny of 'market forces' and rapacious employers.

The underground economy represents a negation of this historic trend. By toiling off the books, workers give up minimum wage and overtime regulations, health insurance, pensions, occupational safety standards – in other words, social security in the broadest sense. This reversal from established rights back to precariousness is the single most important aspect of the growth of informal economic activity. Its implications go far beyond the loss of government revenues, the decline in civic morality and the other aspects of the underground economy that have received most attention. The aim of this final chapter is to explore those implications with respect to the labor movement and the future of social relationships under capitalism.

The 'Italian solution'

Richard Cornuelle wrote in his book *Healing America* that 'to some substantial but unknowable extent, societies everywhere are moving to protect themselves from incompetent governments'.

They are doing this, Cornuelle notes, by creating underground economies that 'can be seen as unplanned, unco-ordinated efforts to protect societies from confused and destructive central authorities'.[1] Cornuelle's championing of this approach, which he calls the 'Italian solution' to the problems of industrial society, is based on an overly sanguine view of the free market. But he is on to something nonetheless. The underground economy is symptomatic of a breakdown of the major institutions of society and the search by people for informal alternatives. It represents an effort by people to achieve more direct satisfaction of needs; it is a turning away from regular business enterprises, government and other established structures in the process of earning a living and getting goods and services. Futurologist Paul Hawken gives this process (both when it is off the books and when it is not) the inelegant but appropriate label of 'disintermediation', which, he has written:

> includes all attempts, both legal and illegal, to circumvent the complicated and cumbersome apparatus of the modern market economy, whether the motive is simple self-gain, the avoidance of a taxable transaction, or the skirting of bureaucratic regulations.[2]

Analysts such as Hawken and Cornuelle see this transformation as the harbinger of a revitalized and scaled down form of capitalism. For them the emergence of mass society, with large bureaucratic structures in both the public and private sectors, was not an inevitable occurrence but rather a deviation that people are now in the process of rectifying. It is difficult to go along with such a revisionist view of the past and rosy view of the future. What is taking place is not a healthy transformation of the system but rather the spread of a variety of arrangements – some satisfactory, some retrograde – by which people are surviving a persistent crisis.

There are signs everywhere that capitalism is moving into a stage in which it requires substantially less human labor in many types of production. Although some new jobs are created – though usually at lower pay and status – in the course of technological change, there are growing numbers of people made permanently redundant. Market economies have always generated 'surplus populations' of unemployed workers who put a check on the power of those still on the job and who can be tapped when the business cycle turns upward. But now there are many people who will find no place in the regular economy even during relative prosperity.

Among other things, the underground economy provides some gainful opportunities for those people who might otherwise have to rely on increasingly unreliable government support. In this sense, the absorption of surplus workers by the informal sector serves the needs of the system very well. It takes some pressure off the state to raise the level of social spending. And it diverts the frustration and anger of the jobless away from challenges to the status quo and into petty transactions and hustles. At the same time, underground suppliers of goods and services often make those commodities available at cheap enough prices so that people in difficult financial conditions can afford them and thus more easily ride out the turbulence of the mainstream economy.

All of this is to say that the informal sector provides new mechanisms for the social reproduction of the labor force. It gives people the material means of subsistence and a psychological sense of purpose at a time when regular institutions are less and less able to perform those roles. It helps people deal with the uncertainty of this time of transition. Yet, ironically, it does so by putting people in activities that are themselves riddled with insecurity and which reproduce many of the unequal relationships of the regular sphere.

Organizing the unorganizable

An attempt to assess the political significance of the underground economy quickly comes up against a problem that has been alluded to repeatedly in the preceding chapters. There are, in effect, two informal economies. The first involves the precarious and exploitative conditions encountered by the weakest members of the labor force, especially blacks, women and immigrants. For them, the underground economy is a realm of oppression; working off the books is a status they are forced into. It is their less than perfect route to survival in a time of economic crisis.

Toiling unofficially and earning undeclared income is, for others, a more rewarding activity. Moonlighters with marketable skills can earn substantial amounts of untaxed income. Some people slip into the underground full-time, finding that this kind of self-employment can make for a comfortable standard of living. It is true that at a certain point, these informal entrepreneurs cross some hazy line and become underground capitalists. They may very well cease to live off their own efforts and profit from the underpaid labor of exploited workers from the other underground economy.

The ambiguous nature of underground activity precludes a unitary political response. As far as the first kind of informal economy is concerned, there is no difficulty in deciding what theoretical position to take. The traditional left-wing principle of organizing the unorganized is still appropriate. The problem is that the ability to carry out that program is severely hampered by the conditions in which informal workers are employed.

The first obstacle is the dispersion of the work-force. A major element of the spread of the underground economy has been the decentralization of production. In an attempt to undermine the power of workers and achieve lower costs and greater flexibility in the labor process, a number of industries have tended to transfer production from larger factories to small workshops where it is easier to keep unions out and operate off the books. In some cases, the work is moved into the home of the worker.

The women doing home labor are among the least powerful of workers. Isolated from one another, they are in a poor position to strive collectively for improvements in pay and working conditions. Where home work is illegal, such as in several industries in the US, there is the added burden of having to remain 'invisible' in order to avoid legal difficulties.

The barriers to organizing this kind of labor force are formidable, but in some places the challenge has been taken up. In Britain a network of organizations has emerged in recent years to support home workers. Taking advantage of the fact that home labor is not illegal in Britain, these groups have focused on informing the workers of their rights. The Leicester Outwork Campaign, for instance, provides advice and advocacy services. In 1984 the group published a package of information relating to tax laws, health and safety regulations, insurance, social security and other matters.[3]

The Leicester group and related organizations have pressed for changes in current British law under which home workers have an ambiguous status combining that of employees and that of self-employed persons. Although many of the home workers are employed off the books, these advocacy groups have sought to obtain full application of labor laws. They have also encouraged the women to contact trade unions, which are generally on record as supporting the organizing of home workers but have made little progress in this regard. Recognizing that much of the home work is being performed by immigrant women, the Leicester campaign and others have published materials in Asian languages, Turkish, Greek and Chinese.

As impressive as the home work campaign in Britain is, the groups involved are essentially offering assistance to individual women rather than creating a collective organization. A different experience in the US suggests the possibilities for 'illegal' workers to act together for improvements in the terms of employment.

For a long time it was assumed that the Mexicans and other Latinos who crossed the US border by the millions in search of work constituted a helpless labor force. Living in fear of arrest and deportation by the immigration authorities, undocumented workers were supposedly prepared to accept the worst sorts of jobs. Many unions saw 'illegals' as a threat, a labor force that could be easily manipulated by unscrupulous employers.

By the late 1970s that image of powerlessness began to dissolve. In October 1977 a group of 200 migrant farmworkers in Arizona could no longer tolerate the miserable conditions in which they toiled. These Mexicans traveled to Arizona every year, crossing the border unofficially and often experiencing grueling journeys through the desert, only to find themselves paid as little as $1 an hour and forced to live in shacks without proper sanitary facilities. The fact that conditions at home were even worse is what prompted them to return season after season.

Supported by an organization called the Maricopa County Organizing Project, the undocumented workers decided to stop working at the height of the picking period for citrus fruits. The ranch they targeted was owned by the brother of conservative Arizona Senator Barry Goldwater.

This, the first strike of undocumented workers in US history, was not without its setbacks. The employer initially used the old tactic of calling in immigration officials to raid the picket line. But eventually, after the walkout spread to other undocumented farmworkers across the state, the company relented and signed a contract with the workers that guaranteed improved wages and conditions.[4]

During the same period, undocumented workers in various parts of the US overcame their fear and began fighting for their rights. Some filed court suits to challenge substandard pay levels and other irregularities. Some of the unions in industries where many 'illegals' worked changed their attitudes towards the undocumented. Rather than making scapegoats of them and supporting measures to tighten up the borders, the union began organizing the foreign workers and challenging the repressive policies of the immigration authorities.

The experience of undocumented worker organizing is not an exact precedent for the underground economy. Most of the companies making use of 'illegals' were not themselves operating outside the law – there was no prohibition against hiring undocumented workers – and the firms were usually on the books, as were many of the 'illegals'. Yet the successes in Arizona and elsewhere do indicate that workers who are in some way outside the law can still find ways to fight against oppression.

Workers without chains?

It would be a bit too optimistic, however, to suggest that organizing and collective action among clandestine and dispersed workers can easily become the rule rather than the exception. Often it is the fear of detection that inhibits the informal worker from joining with others to improve his or her lot. Yet there is more to it than that.

First of all, the fact that informal work involves certain violations of law requires that the worker enter into a kind of conspiracy with the employer to cheat the government. Sweatshop workers, for instance, may hardly be willing participants in this 'plot', but they often have to go along if they want to keep the job. For better-paid underground employees, there may indeed be a relationship of genuine collusion rather than antagonism with the boss.

When the underground activity takes the form of self-employment, the inclination toward collective action is even weaker. Although the 'autonomous' status of these people may often be merely a legal fiction, they do not have easy access to the mechanisms by which workers address their grievances. In fact it is all too easy for these informal sector participants to see themselves as individual entrepreneurs and thus succumb to the ideology of self-initiative that is being promoted so vigorously these days. This may be true even as the classic syndrome of self-employment – that it translates into self-exploitation – appears in the informal economy. Stuart Henry, an analyst of the underground economy, has aptly stated that 'the best interests of capitalism are served when people have a degree of autonomy over their lives'.[5]

That desire for autonomy cannot be totally written off as self-delusion. Despite the economic turmoil of the past dozen years, there continue to be people who seek a life not dominated by a permanent, full-time job. Some of them, particularly among the young, are prepared to tolerate insecurity in the effort to escape from the career-job trap.

Several years ago, the French magazine, *Le Nouvel Observateur*, used the phrase 'workers without chains' to refer to the apparently significant numbers of young people who preferred to work intermittently at jobs that were usually off the books: 'They want to be free and available. They prefer insecurity to dependence, risk to routine, the unexpected to habit. They choose to work how and when they please'.[6]

There are, to be sure, drawbacks to the life of the voluntary marginal worker. A few well-situated people may be able to live well off the books, but for most the price of this relative freedom is an inadequate level of income. The young and unattached may not mind living this way for a while, but a life of odd jobs and the absence of social security are likely to lose their appeal as one grows older.

In one of his more utopian moments, Marx imagined post-capitalist life in the following terms:

Nobody has an exclusive sphere of activity but each can become accomplished in any branch he wishes, [and] society regulates the general production and thus makes it possible for me to do one thing today and another tomorrow, to hunt in the morning, fish in the afternoon, rear cattle in the evening, criticize after dinner, just as I have a mind, without ever becoming a hunter, fisherman, shepherd or critic.[7]

Today we face a society that hardly manages to 'regulate' and guarantee the 'general production', and thus the need for people to work at defined jobs is far from obsolete. Yet it may be that the underground economy offers, at least for some people, the closest thing available to that free choice of activity. The enhanced flexibility and variety that informal work can provide may outweigh the negative aspects of marginality and insecurity. It does not compare with the traditional left-wing vision of a completely free and abundant society, but it does have the advantage of being readily available.

Perhaps the informal economy does, after all, include a political nuance in the use of the term 'underground'. Rather than being mere survival or dishonesty or exploitation, informal work potentially represents a struggle for change. People are rejecting, to the extent they are able, both the regimentation of the economic system when it is functioning well and the dislocations when it is not. This is, admittedly, a complex form of resistance: it is unorganized and in some ways not antagonistic to the structures it is opposing.

Yet beneath the contradictory features there are signs of a search for an alternative way of life in a system that remains crisis-ridden but resistant to fundamental political change. The underground economy may yet provide the basis for social autonomy.

Appendix: Estimating the underground labor force

Attempts to measure the size of the underground labor force have come up against the same difficulties that have plagued efforts to estimate underground GNP (see chapter 4). Given the clandestine nature of the phenomenon, the people involved are as hard to count as the dollars or sterling that circulate in it. Nevertheless, efforts have been made.

A 1983 study by the International Labour Office reviewed the estimates that had been calculated throughout the developed capitalist countries. The numbers ranged from as little as three per cent of the official labor force in France up to 40 per cent in Norway; but different analyses gave substantially different results even within a single country.[1]

It is not clear what these estimates are worth, based as they are on a potpourri of polls, derivations from underground GNP estimates, analyses of changes in official labor force data, and 'off the cuff' statements by journalists and government officials.

The most valid research relates to attempts to find traces of the underground labor force in the official employment statistics compiled by governments. One technique used in the US is to look for significant discrepancies between the two methods used to calculate the numbers of jobs and jobholders. The Census Bureau's Current Population Survey (CPS) includes monthly questioning of a sample of some 60,000 households about the work activity of their members. Everyone is categorized as employed, unemployed or not in the labor force. The Bureau of Labor Statistics (BLS) separately surveys about 189,000 establishments of all sizes to determine the number of people on official payrolls.

The attempt to use the two series for underground measurement purposes is based on the assumption that people doing informal work will describe themselves (or be described by the householder member interviewed) as employed when CPS data-gatherers come to visit. Such persons who did not also hold regular jobs would not appear in the BLS survey, which only covers on-the-books employees in above-ground firms. A rise in the CPS measure of employment relative to the BLS one would suggest an expansion of participation in the underground economy.[2]

Unfortunately, various analyses of the two series have yielded contradictory results. Edward Denison of the US Bureau of Economic Analysis performed the exercise and concluded there had been no unusual divergences between the two series from 1947 to 1979 and thus no evidence of an expanding underground work-force.[3] Making certain adjustments to the data, David O'Neill of the US Census Bureau did detect a slight upward tendency in the CPS measure relative to the BLS one and used this to assert the existence of 1.7 million full-time underground workers in 1981.[4] The problem with this method is the need to assert a normal relationship between the two series in order to claim that a change in the ratio is a reflection of increasing off-the-books employment.

There is also a problem in assuming any consistent type of response to household survey questions by people who are working off the books. There is just as much reason to assume that an informal worker will describe himself or herself as unemployed (especially if one is collecting unemployment benefits at the time) or not in the labor force (if one is collecting disability pay or some other benefit intended for someone not able to work) as there is to think the response will be 'employed'. Survey results could be skewed in any number of possible ways.

Denison, determined to defend the integrity of official statistics, claimed to have resolved this problem by tracking the relationship between the two employment series and the overall population. He found a consistent relationship between each of the series and the total number of people in the US over the age of 14, back to 1947.[5] What Denison ignored is that figures on the general population are as controversial as those on the labor force. It is quite possible – and so has it been argued frequently – that millions of people can be missed by the decennial censuses, particularly inner-city residents who are likely to be participants in some underground activities. Moreover, even if Denison was correct, his conclusions proved nothing about the numbers of off-the-books workers who also held regular jobs.

Another approach to the measurement issue is to examine the various categories of statistics on the official labor force and look for extraordinary increases among those groups most likely to engage in underground labor. Drawing definite conclusions from this analysis again requires the assumption of predictable survey responses by informal workers; but the trends can suggest the general magnitude of the *potential* labor force for the underground economy. Using this approach, Italian economists have estimated that as many as five million people in that country work exclusively off the books and another two million people with regular jobs also have undeclared second occupations. This is in a country with an official labor force of about 20 million. (For more on Italy, see chapter 7.)

Economists in the US and the UK have been more concerned with estimating the underground gross national product, so there has been little analysis of the numbers of people working off the books. The following pages look at what the official labor force data in the two countries suggest.

Moonlighters

The assumption in many countries, more so in Europe than in North America, is that anyone who works a second job is doing so off the books. Many articles have not hesitated to use 'moon-lighting' interchangeably with 'informal labor'. While this may be appropriate for countries such as Italy where part-time work has been largely prohibited, it is not valid for the US and the UK.

In the US there has been a substantial amount of multiple-job-holding for many years, the conventional wisdom being that married men earning low wages in their primary job had to look for additional work to meet family financial obligations. The proportion of employed persons reporting that they held more than one job has remained fairly constant at about five per cent since the early 1960s. Yet as the labor force has increased, this constant percentage has come to represent a larger absolute number of people. That number rose from 4.0 to 4.8 million from 1970 to 1980 (the most recent data available).

In Britain the statistics are more limited. Data on moonlighting started to be collected much later than in the US, and the figures for the 1970s come from three different sources (the General Household Survey, the Family Expenditure Survey and the EEC Labor Force Survey) that are not consistent in timing and methodology.[6] It is not possible to derive a clear trend line.

Part-time workers in primary jobs
The rise in part-time work during the 1970s was mainly attributable to the entry into the labor market of many women whose domestic responsibilities prevented them from working full-time outside the home. In the US, though not Britain, there was also a significant increase in male part-time work during the decade. Many of the people working less than full-time were employed by the service industries, which expanded rapidly during this period and frequently made use of labor in irregular schedules.

It can be argued that many of the people doing part-time work in a regular job, whether voluntarily or because there was no full-time work to be found, were in a position to do additional labor off the books. It is also possible that some of the part-time jobs reported to government interviewers were themselves in the informal economy.

In the US, the total number of part-time workers rose from 11.7 million in 1970 to nearly 16 million in 1982, with women accounting for two-thirds of the increase. In Britain, the number of part-timers increased from 3.8 million in 1971 to 4.5 million in 1981, with women accounting for *all* of the rise (the number of male part-timers actually declined in that period).

The self-employed
Another school of thought holds that full-time underground workers are likely to describe themselves as self-employed when surveyed.

In the US the ranks of the self-employed increased by 30 per cent from 1970 to 1983, representing a rise of 2.1 million people. In Britain there was an increase of about 300,000 self-employed persons from the early 1970s to 1983.

Non-participants in the labor force
The second most important trend in the labor markets of many

advanced capitalist countries over the past 15 years (after the rise of female participation in the paid work-force) has been the decline of male participation rates. The latter has been a less dramatic trend, but the statistics indicate that a steadily growing number of adult men are not holding regular jobs. Even when the effects of longer schooling and earlier retirement are taken into account, the trend is significant.

It is likely that many of the adult men who report themselves as being outside the labor force (including some pensioners) are actually doing work that is off the books. In the Census Bureau study cited above, O'Neill looked at the number of 'prime working age' males outside the labor force and concluded that in 1981 more than one million of them in the US were actually doing undeclared work. His analysis was based in part on reports that a large number of men receiving federal disability payments – the eligibility criteria for which were eased during the 1970s – work at least part-time off the books.[7]

The number of non-participants in the US labor force, both male and female, rose by more than 8 million from 1970 to 1983. In Britain the increase was about one million.

The unemployed

This is a segment of the labor force whose members are clearly in a position to work off the books while waiting to return to a regular job. Extra unofficial income is usually necessary to supplement inadequate unemployment benefits. Given the periodic campaigns in both the US and the UK against supposed abuses of the unemployment benefit system, it is very likely that people receiving these payments report themselves as unemployed in government surveys (the responses to which are supposed to be confidential), regardless of what they are doing on the side.

The size of the jobless population, while cyclical, reached extraordinarily high levels in both the US and Britain during the 1970s and 1980s. In the US, the ranks of the unemployed rose from about 4 million in 1970 to more than 10 million and remained at that level even during the economic recovery of the early 1980s. In Britain the economy did not enjoy much of a recovery in 1983 and 1984, and by the middle of that latter year, the redundant population surpassed three million, compared with less than one million in 1972.

Illegal immigrants

Even before the underground economy became a subject of frequent discussion, people used to talk about a clandestine labor market in the US and some other countries consisting of foreigners who worked without government authorization. The number of illegal foreign workers was greatest in those European countries that ended their 'guest worker' programs during the 1970s and sought to coerce the immigrants to return to their native countries by taking away their work permits.[8] In Britain the immigrant population continued to grow during the 1970s, but relatively few of the people were 'illegal', since firmer rights of residence were given to migrants from the countries of the New Commonwealth and Pakistan. These rights, however, were later weakened by successive government nationality acts.

The number of 'illegal aliens' has been a hotly contested issue in the US for many years. Before anyone was concerned with the informal economy, this was the main arena of activity for social scientists inclined to count the uncountable. Since 1970 about a dozen major studies have put the number of undocumented foreign workers anywhere from two million to 10 million.[9]

For a long time it was assumed that undocumented workers toiled off the books, since they and their employers wanted to keep their status hidden, and because the foreigners would not be in a position later to collect federal retirement benefits. Yet once researchers began to conduct careful interviews among aliens apprehended by the immigration authorities, it was found that the majority of them did have taxes withheld from their pay. A series of studies found that as much as 88 per cent of undocumented workers were working *on* the books.[10] Government officials began to realize that the undocumented workers were actually making a net financial contribution to society, since the taxes they were paying probably far outweighed the value of the public services they were taking advantage of.[11]

In its study of unreported income, the Internal Revenue Service assessed the role of undocumented workers in the US underground economy by assuming that there were about two to six million of them in the country in 1979. They were estimated to have earned a maximum of $29 billion in wages, but only about $8 billion of that was thought to be off the books, and the tax loss to the IRS could have been less than $1 billion[12] – for a year in which the agency estimated the total legal-sector 'tax gap' at more than $60 billion.

The potential underground labor force

The increases from the beginning of the 1970s to the early 1980s in those employment categories that indicate the size of the underground labor force amount to the following (figures are in millions):

	United States	United Kingdom
Moonlighters	0.8	not available
Part-timers	4.2	0.7
The self-employed	2.1	0.3
Non-participants	8.4	1.0
The unemployed	6.6	2.3
Illegal immigrants	4.0	not available
	26.1	**4.3**

It is not realistic to suggest that anything like 100 per cent of these increases reflect underground activity. A reasonable guess in most cases would be that about half do. For undocumented workers in the US, if four million is used as the estimate for the total numbers, then about one million, or one-quarter, are likely to be working off the books. This means that a very rough approximation of the underground labor force in the US would be 12 million. In Britain the figure could be put at about 2.5 million, adding in a few hundred thousand to account for growth in the numbers of moonlighters and illegal immigrants working in the informal economy.

These estimates, while hardly rigorous (rigor being impossible in this context), suggest a magnitude of underground labor that is in keeping with impressionistic evidence. In the case of each country, the figures for off-the-books workers amount to about 10 per cent of the official labor force. Such a figure is large enough to be significant yet not so great as to suggest that the informal economy is overtaking the regular one. Ten per cent is also consistent with the conclusions that are reached in chapter 4 regarding the size of the underground gross national product.

However, given the shakiness of these numbers, it is perhaps best to conclude on a less specific quantitative note. What seems safest to say is that more people than ever before have a need or desire to change the way they work and are finding underground activity a vital part of that process.

Notes

2. The fragmentation of work

1. 'Unreported work may cost US billions in taxes and impair plans', *New York Times*, 15 January 1978.
2. *Report of the National Advisory Commission on Civil Disorders*, New York: Bantam Books 1968, especially pp. 251–65.
3. *The Scarman Report: The Brixton Disorders, 10–12 April 1981*, Harmondsworth: Penguin 1982, especially pp. 33–6.
4. See the review of the literature in David Gordon, *Theories of Poverty and Unemployment*, Lexington, Massachusetts: D.C. Heath 1972.
5. See *ibid* and David Gordon, Richard Edwards and Michael Reich, *Segmented Work, Divided Workers*, Cambridge: Cambridge University Press 1982.
6. Stanley Friedlander, *Unemployment in the Urban Core*, New York: Praeger 1972, p. 182.
7. 'The army and the jobless' (editorial), *Wall Street Journal*, 29 April 1977.
8. See, for example, Bob Kuttner, 'The declining middle', *The Atlantic*, July 1983.
9. For the US, see Stanley Nollen, *New Work Schedules in Practice*, New York: Van Nostrand Reinhold 1982; for Britain, see Anne Phillips, *Hidden Hands*, London: Pluto Press 1983.
10. See, for example, 'Temp work becomes full-time way of life', *New York Times*, 17 October 1982.
11. Quoted in 'A profile of the temporary help industry and its workers', *Monthly Labor Review*, May 1974, p. 44.
12. See Roger Moore, 'Aspects of segmentation in the United Kingdom building industry labour market', in Frank Wilkinson (ed.), *The Dynamics of Labour Market Segmentation*, London: Academic Press 1981.
13. See 'Gypsy scholars roam the academic landscape', *New York Times*, 10 January 1982.
14. Bernard Lefkowitz, *Breaktime: Living Without Work in a Nine-to-Five*

World, Harmondsworth: Penguin 1980.

15. 'The great male cop-out from the work ethic', *Business Week*, 14 November 1977.

16. By the end of the 1970s more than one-third of all US households received some kind of federal benefit. See 'Census finds US benefits reach 1 out of 3 families', *New York Times*, 13 March 1981.

17. Quoted in Irwin Ross, 'Why the underground economy is booming', *Fortune*, 9 October 1978.

3. The tax revolt and the sweatshop

1. *Revenue Statistics of OECD Member Countries*, Paris: Organisation for Economic Co-operation and Development 1982, pp. 73–4.

2. See 'Despite Reagan cuts, many are taxed more', *New York Times*, 15 April 1983.

3. Enzo Mingione, 'Capitalist crisis, neo-dualism and marginalization', *International Journal of Urban and Regional Research*, Vol. 2, No.2, June 1978.

4. For a discussion of the economics of subcontracting, see Andrew Friedman, *Industry and Labour*, London: Macmillan 1977, pp. 118–29.

5. 'Japan: the world's biggest cottage industry', *Economist*, 26 July 1980.

6. Robert Wood, 'Japan's multitier wage system', *Forbes*, 18 August 1980. See also Michael McAbee, 'Pebbles support Japan's monolith', *Industry Week*, 1 May 1978.

7. 'Subcontracting: be your own boss', *Economist*, 4 June 1983.

8. *The Return of the Sweatshop*, a report by New York State Senator Franz Leichter, 26 February 1981, p. 3. See also 'After years of decline, sweatshops are back', *New York Times*, 12 October 1983; and a four-part series called 'Sweatshops: the new slavery' in the *New York Daily News*, 9–12 December 1980.

9. Barbro Hoel, 'Contemporary clothing sweatshops, Asian female labour and collective organisation', in Jackie West (ed.), *Work, Women and the Labour Market*, London: Routledge & Kegan Paul 1982, p. 85.

10. See Stephen Castles, *Here for Good: Western Europe's New Ethnic Minorities*, London: Pluto Press 1984.

11. Among the writings on home work are Sheila Allen, 'Production and reproduction: the lives of women homeworkers', *Sociological Review*, Vol. 31, No. 4, November 1983; Simon Crine, *The Hidden Army*, London: Low Pay Unit 1979; and Carla Lipsig-Mummé, 'La renaissance du travail à domicile dans les économies développées,

Sociologie du Travail, No. 3, 1983.

12. Catherine Hakim, 'Homeworking in the London clothing industry', *Employment Gazette*, September 1982; Marilyn Webb, 'Sweatshops for one: the rise in industrial homework', *Village Voice*, 10–16 February 1982. See also Hardy Green and Elizabeth Weiner, 'Bringing it all back home', *In These Times*, 11–17 March 1981.

13. Webb, *op. cit.*

14. Catherine Hakim, 'Homework and outwork: national estimates from two surveys', *Employment Gazette*, January 1984.

15. See, for example, Floya Anthias, 'Sexual divisions and ethnic adaptation: the case of Greek-Cypriot women', in Annie Phizacklea (ed.), *One Way Ticket: Migration and Female Labour*, London: Routledge & Kegan Paul 1983.

16. For a candid view of Silicon Valley, see Lenny Siegel, 'Down in Silicon Valley', *Multinational Monitor*, April 1983; Robert Howard, 'Second class in Silicon Valley', *Working Papers*, September–October 1981; and Lenny Siegel and John Markoff, 'The hazards of high tech', *Environmental Action*, July–August 1981.

17. John Markoff, 'California's space-age sweatshops', *Los Angeles Times*, 28 October 1980.

18. 'Black market in Silicon Valley: an underground of cheap labor', *San Jose Sunday Mercury News*, 31 August 1980.

19. See Rebecca Morales, 'Cold solder on a hot stove', in Jan Zimmerman (ed.), *The Technological Woman: Interfacing with Tomorrow*, New York: Praeger 1983; and Naomi Katz and David Kemnitzer, 'Fast forward: the internationalization of Silicon Valley', in June Nash and María Patricia Fernández-Kelly (eds.), *Women, Men and the International Division of Labor*, Albany: State University of New York Press 1983.

20. Quoted in Philip Mattera, 'Home computer sweatshops', *The Nation*, 2 April 1983. See also Ursula Huws, 'New technology homeworkers', *Employment Gazette*, January 1984 and the same author's *The New Homeworkers*, London: Low Pay Unit 1984.

21. Alvin Toffler, *The Third Wave*, New York: William Morrow 1980.

4. Measuring the unmeasurable

1. 'What ever happened to the cashless society?' *Morgan Guaranty Survey*, February 1972, p. 13.

2. 'The growing appetite for cash', *Business Conditions* (Federal Reserve Bank of Chicago), April 1971, p. 16.

3. James Henry, 'Calling in the big bills', *Washington Monthly*, May 1976; the econometric details were given in an earlier unpublished

paper entitled 'The currency connection: a modest proposal for attacking crime in America'.

4. Peter Gutmann, 'The subterranean economy', *Financial Analysts Journal*, November–December 1977.

5. See Gillian Garcia, 'The currency ratio and the subterranean economy', *Financial Analysts Journal*, November–December 1978 as well as various chapters of Vito Tanzi (ed.), *The Underground Economy in the United States and Abroad*, Lexington, Massachusetts: D.C. Heath 1982. Gutmann's technique also turned out to be less than completely original. The ratio of currency to demand deposits was previously studied by Phillip Cagan in *Determinants and Effects of Changes in the Stock of Money, 1875–1960*, New York: National Bureau of Economic Research 1965. Finally, it should be noted that a Gutmann-type analysis of the UK yielded inconclusive results. See Michael O'Higgins, 'Aggregate measures of tax evasion', *British Tax Review*, No. 5, 1981.

6. The leading example of this is the work of International Monetary Fund economist Vito Tanzi. Two of his articles are contained in Tanzi (ed.), *op. cit.* See also his 'The underground economy in the United States: annual estimates, 1930–80', *IMF Staff Papers*, Vol. 20, No. 2, June 1983.

7. Edgar Feige, 'How big is the irregular economy?', *Challenge*, November–December 1979. This original article was found to be seriously flawed. Richard Porter of the Federal Reserve carried out Feige's calculations year by year back to 1939 (Feige himself had only done 1939, 1976 and 1978) and found that they yielded *negative* values for the size of the underground economy in virtually every year. See Porter's unpublished paper, 'Some notes on estimating the under-ground economy', August 1979. Feige revised his technique in a way that eliminated the minus signs for earlier years and reached essentially the same conclusions for the late 1970s. See his unpublished paper, 'A new perspective on macroeconomic phenomena', 1980.

8. Kerrick Macafee, 'A glimpse of the hidden economy in the national accounts', *Economic Trends*, No. 316, February 1980; also in Tanzi (ed.), *op. cit.*

9. Andrew Dilnot and C.N. Morris, 'What do we know about the black economy in the United Kingdom?', *Fiscal Studies*, Vol.2, No.1, March 1981; also in Tanzi (ed.), *op. cit.*

10. In the US the analogous discrepancy between different ways of calculating national output has been extremely low, less than 1 per cent of GNP. See the testimony of Robert Parker of the Bureau of Economic Analysis in US Congress, House Committee on Ways and Means, Subcommittee on Oversight, *Underground Economy*, Hearings

held 16 July, 10 September, 9 and 11 October 1979, Washington: Government Printing Office 1980. Some attention has also been paid in the US to discrepancies between the two measures of income: Internal Revenue Service data on adjusted gross income from tax returns and personal income data from the national accounts. Yet the technical differences between the two series make it difficult to derive any conclusions about the magnitude of unreported income. See the articles by Thae Park in the November 1981 and April 1983 issues of *Survey of Current Business*.

11. For a full description of the TCMP, see Appendix C of US Internal Revenue Service, *Estimates of Income Unreported on Individual Income Tax Returns*, Washington: Government Printing Office 1979.

12. *Ibid* and US Internal Revenue Service, *Income Tax Compliance Research: Estimates for 1973–1981*, Washington: Government Printing Office 1983.

13. A summary of the informal supplier research can be found in the 1983 IRS report, Appendix D. The full study is Survey Research Center, Institute for Social Research, University of Michigan at Ann Arbor, *The Measurement of Selected Income Flows in Informal Markets*, December 1982.

14. IRS 1983 report, Appendix B, p. 62.

5. The underground and the underworld

1. Sir Leon Radzinowicz and Joan King, *The Growth of Crime*, New York: Basic Books 1977, pp. 4–5.

2. *A Handbook on White Collar Crime: Everyone's Problem, Everyone's Loss*, Washington: US Chamber of Commerce 1974.

3. President's Commission on Law Enforcement and Administration of Justice, *Task Force Report: Crime and its Impact – An Assessment*, Washington: Government Printing Office 1967, pp. 43–53.

4. US Internal Revenue Service, *Income Tax Compliance Research: Estimates for 1973–1981*, Washington: Government Printing Office 1983, p. 39.

5. US Congress, Senate Committee on Governmental Affairs, Permanent Subcommittee on Investigations, *Illegal Narcotics Profits*, Hearings held 7, 11, 12, 13 and 14 December 1979, Washington: Government Printing Office 1980, pp. 393–6.

6. *Ibid*, p. 118.

7. On cash laundering, see Penny Lernoux, *In Banks We Trust*, New York: Doubleday 1984; and Howard Kohn, 'Cocaine: you can bank on it', *Esquire*, October 1983.

8. US Congress, Senate Committee on Governmental Affairs, Permanent

Subcommittee on Investigations, *Crime and Secrecy: The Use of Offshore Banks and Companies*, Washington: Government Printing Office 1983, p. 15.

9. The study is reprinted in *Illegal Narcotics Profits, op. cit.*, p. 473.

10. *Crime and Secrecy, op. cit.*, p. 16.

11. See Jonathan Kwitney, *Vicious Circles: The Mafia in the Marketplace*, New York: W.W. Norton 1979.

12. See Jason Ditton, 'Perks, pilferage and the fiddle: the historical structure of invisible wages', *Theory and Society*, Vol.4, No. 1, 1977.

13. Stuart Henry, *The Hidden Economy: The Context and Control of Borderline Crime*, London: Martin Robertson 1978, p. ix.

14. *Policing the Hidden Economy: The Significance and Control of Fiddles*, London: Outer Circle Policy Unit 1978, p. 2.

15. See note 8 of chapter 4.

16. Gerald Mars, *Cheats at Work: An Anthropology of Workplace Crime*, London: Allen & Unwin 1983, chapter 8.

17. 'Survey contends that "time theft" costs US billions', *Miami Herald*, 20 December 1982.

18. For instance, new telecommunications equipment makes it easier for employers to monitor telephones for unauthorized calls by employees. See 'Personal use of company phones is target of cost-cutting efforts', *Wall Street Journal*, 11 April 1984.

19. 'Organized bootlegging of cigarets is battled by northern states hurt by tax-revenue loss', *Wall Street Journal*, 15 September 1976.

20. Carl Simon and Ann Witte, *Beating the System: the Underground Economy*, Boston: Auburn House 1982, p. 48.

21. See Jonathan Fenby, *Piracy and the Public*, London: Frederick Muller 1983.

22. 'Fighting the counterfeiters', *Times*, 27 October 1983.

23. See Louis Kraar, 'Fighting the fakes from Taiwan', *Fortune*, 30 May 1983; and 'The capital of counterfeiting', *Dun's Review*, October 1978.

6. The government's dilemma

1. US General Accounting Office, *Who's Not Filing Income Tax Returns?*, Washington, 1979.

2. See 'Private computers' income data to aid IRS in hunt for evaders', *New York Times*, 29 August 1983; 'IRS starts hunt for tax evaders, using mail-order concerns' lists', *New York Times*, 25 December 1983; and the testimony of IRS Commissioner Roscoe Egger in US Congress, Senate Committee on Governmental Affairs, Subcommittee on Oversight of Government Management, *Computer Matching: Taxpayer Records*, Hearing held 6 June 1984, Washington: Govern-

ment Printing Office 1984.

3. UK Parliament, Committee on Enforcement Powers of the Revenue Departments, *Report*, London: Her Majesty's Stationery Office 1983.

4. UK Inland Revenue, *Report for the Year ended 31st December 1983*, London: Her Majesty's Stationery Office 1984, p. 28; 'More lost tax recovered by Revenue', *Financial Times*, 4 April 1984; and 'The electronic taxman comes', *Economist*, 28 July 1984.

5. James Henry, 'Calling in the big bills', *Washington Monthly*, May 1976.

6. 'The $100 cure for crime', *Economist*, 4 September 1982.

7. On Israel, see 'Shekel made Israel's currency; drive planned on black market', *New York Times*, 23 February 1980; on Nigeria, see 'Naira restrictions and reactions', *West Africa*, 14 May 1984.

8. Gabriel Tahar, *Le Marché du travail marginal et clandestin en France, au Royaume-Uni et en Italie*, Commission of the European Community, February 1980, p. 95.

9. Reagan's radio address of 24 April 1982 was reprinted in the *Weekly Compilation of Presidential Documents*, 30 April 1982, p. 527.

10. Reagan's State of the Union address was reprinted in the *New York Times*, 26 January 1984.

11. George Gilder, *Wealth and Poverty*, New York: Basic Books 1981, p. 17.

12. Geoffrey Howe, 'New directions for the British economy', a speech delivered at a *Financial Times* conference in July 1979 and reprinted in *Vital Speeches of the Day*, 1 September 1979.

13. For an account and defense of this doctrine, see Jude Wanniski, *The Way the World Works*, New York: Simon and Schuster 1978.

14. 'The quiet repeal of the corporate income tax', *New York Times*, 2 August 1981.

15. The following section draws heavily from Philip Mattera, 'From the runaway shop to the sweatshop: enterprise zones and the redevelopment of the cities', *Radical America*, Vol. 15, No. 5, September–October 1981.

16. James Anderson, 'Back to the 19th century', *New Statesman*, 11 July 1980.

17. Stuart Butler, 'For enterprise zones', *New York Times*, 13 June 1980.

18. Stuart Butler, 'Urban renewal: a modest proposal', *Policy Review*, No. 13, Summer 1980. See also the same author's *Enterprise Zones: Greenlining the Inner Cities*, New York: Universe Books 1981.

19. 'Reagan calls his version "urban enterprise zones"', *New York Times*, 23 November 1980.

20. 'Enterprise zones draw mixed reviews', *Washington Post*, 19 June 1981.

21. See, for example, 'States prove more "enterprising" ', *Business Week*, 29 November 1982; and 'States expand enterprise zones despite lack of federal incentives', *Wall Street Journal*, 31 July 1984.

22. See Jane Houlton and Fiona Mallon, 'Erroneous zones', *New Statesman*, 20 August 1982; 'UK enterprise zones seem successful but depend largely on government aid', *Wall Street Journal*, 29 April 1983; and John Shutt, 'Tory enterprise zones and the labour movement', *Capital and Class*, No. 23, Summer 1984.

23. See Dave Spooner, 'Freeports in the UK', *International Labour Reports*, No. 1, January–February 1984.

24. Walter Williams, 'Government-sanctioned restraints that reduce economic opportunities for minorities', *Policy Review*, No. 2, Fall 1977.

25. Quoted in 'Reagan's wish is no minimum wage for youth', *New York Times*, 10 February 1983.

26. For an account of these events, see Jonathan Rauch, 'Anatomy of a regulatory proposal – the battle over industrial homework', *National Journal*, 6 June 1981, p. 1013.

27. Gilder, *op. cit.*, p. 27.

28. David Talbot, 'Fast times for high-tech: meet the moguls who are reprogramming our future', *Mother Jones*, December 1983.

29. See Susie Hughes, 'Enterprise allowance scheme – the pioneers', *Employment Gazette*, December 1983.

30. Peter Gutmann, 'The grand unemployment illusion', *Journal of the Institute of Socioeconomic Studies*, Vol. 4, No. 2, Summer 1979, p. 22.

31. Carl Simon and Ann Witte, *Beating the System: the Underground Economy*, Boston: Auburn House 1982, p. xv.

7. The submerged economy in Italy

1. This chapter draws heavily on Philip Mattera, 'Small is not beautiful: decentralized production and the underground economy in Italy', *Radical America*, Vol. 14, No. 5, September–October 1980.

2. See, for example, Massimo Paci, *Mercato del lavoro e classi sociali in Italia*, Bologna: Il Mulino 1973; Luigi Frey, 'Le piccole e medie imprese industriali di fronte al mercato di lavoro in Italia', *Inchiesta*, No. 14, April–June 1974; Centro studi investimenti sociali (CENSIS), *L'occupazione occulta: caratteristiche della partecipazione al lavoro in Italia*, Rome 1976; Istituto di Sociologia, Università di Torino, *Lavorare due volte: una ricerca pilota sul secondo lavoro*, Turin: Book Store 1979; and Daniela del Boca and Francesco Forte, 'Recent empirical surveys and theoretical interpretations of the parallel economy in Italy', in Vito Tanzi (ed.), *The Underground Economy in*

the United States and Abroad, Lexington, Massachusetts: D.C. Heath 1982.

3. See Andrea Saba, *L'industria sommersa: il nuovo modello di sviluppo*, Venice: Marsilio 1980; and Antonio Martino, 'Measuring Italy's underground economy', *Policy Review*, Spring 1981.

4. The earliest works include Luigi Frey, 'Il lavoro a domicilio in Lombardia', *Relazioni Sociali*, No. 11–12, 1971 (reprinted in Paolo Leon and Marco Marocchi (eds.), *Sviluppo economico italiano e forza-lavoro*, Padua: Marsilio 1973); Sebastiano Brusco, 'Prime note per uno studio del lavoro a domicilio in Italia', *Inchiesta*, No. 10, April–June 1973; and an entire issue of the union journal, *Quaderni di Rassegna Sindacale*, No. 44–5, September–December 1973.

5. The best English-language sources on this period are, in Britain, the volumes published by Red Notes, including *Working-Class Autonomy and the Crisis*; and in the US, two special issues of *Radical America*, Vol. 5, No. 5, September–October 1971 and Vol. 7, No. 2, March–April 1973.

6. The Italian literature on decentralization is huge. See, for example, Luigi Frey, 'La problematica del decentramento produttivo', *Economia e Politica Industriale*, No. 6, April–June 1974; Federazione Lavoratori Metalmeccanici (FLM) di Bergamo (ed.), *Sindacato e piccola impresa*, Bari: De Donato 1975; Clara de Marco and Manlio Talamo, *Lavoro nero: decentramento produttivo e lavoro a domicilio*, Milan: Mazzotta 1977; R. Brunetta and others, *L'Impresa in frantumi*, Rome: Editrice Sindacale Italiana 1980. See also the excellent article by Fergus Murray, 'The decentralisation of production – the decline of the mass collective worker?', *Capital and Class*, No. 19, Spring 1983.

7. Frey, 'Le piccole e medie imprese', *op. cit.*

8. Sebastiano Brusco, 'Organizzazione del lavoro e decentramento produttivo nel settore metalmeccanico', in FLM di Bergamo (ed.), *op. cit.*

9. See, for example, 'Dietro i miracoli della città-azienda', *Corriere della Sera*, 22 October 1979.

10. Paul Lewis, 'The Pratos of Italy: oases of hard work', *New York Times*, 16 March 1980; 'A family called Brambilla', *Time*, 7 April 1980. See also Barbara Ellis, 'Italy's prosperous anarchy', *Forbes*, 2 April 1979.

11. See the works cited in note 4, De Marco and Talamo, *op. cit.* and Maria Rosa Cutrufelli, *Operaie senza fabbrica: inchiesta sul lavoro a domicilio*, Rome: Riuniti 1977.

12. Frey, 'Il lavoro a domicilio', *op. cit.* and the same author's 'Dal lavoro a domicilio al decentramento dell'attività produttiva', in *Quaderni di*

Rassegna Sindacale, op. cit. All subsequent work on the subject has taken Frey's estimates as authoritative.

13. Brusco, 'Prime note', *op. cit.*

14. Karl Marx, *Capital*, Vol. 1, chapter XV, section 8.

15. Clara de Marco and Manlio Talamo, 'Bambini operai ed economia sommersa', *Fabbrica Aperta*, June–July 1979. See also Andriano Baglivo, *Il mercato dei bambini*, Milan: Feltrinelli 1980; and Marina Valcarenghi, *Child Labour in Italy*, London: Anti-Slavery Society 1981. Child labor is also a problem in Britain; see Emma MacLennan, *Child Labour in London*, London: Low Pay Unit 1982.

16. De Marco and Talamo, *Lavoro nero, op. cit.*, pp. 93–4.

17. CENSIS, *La presenza dei lavoratori stranieri in Italia*, Rome 1978. The later estimate is cited in Raffaele Lungarella, 'L'immigrazione straniera in Emilia-Romagna', *Inchiesta*, No. 59–60, January–June 1983.

18. See CENSIS, *L'occupazione occulta, op. cit.* and Istituto di Sociologia, *op. cit.*

19. Saba, *op. cit.*, p. 19.

20. Del Boca and Forte, *op. cit.*, p. 193.

21. 'Il metalmezzadro protagonista dell'economia sommersa al Sud', *Corriere della Sera*, 15 October 1979.

22. 'Small companies fuel the Italian economy', *Wall Street Journal*, 12 April 1982. For a general discussion in English of the more 'advanced' form of the submerged economy, see Sebastiano Brusco, 'The Emilian model: productive decentralisation and social integration', *Cambridge Journal of Economics*, Vol. 6, No. 2, June 1982.

23. Augusto Graziani, Introduction to Alfredo Del Monte and Mario Raffa (eds.), *Tecnologia e decentramento produttivo*, Turin: Rosenberg & Sellier 1977, p. 21.

24. Giorgio Amendola, 'Interrogativi sul caso Fiat', *Rinascita*, 9 November 1979.

25. 'Una rivista per gli imprenditori democratici', *Orientamenti Nuovi per la Piccola e Media Industria*, No. 7–8, July–August 1979.

26. Paolo Cantelli, *L'economia sommersa*, Rome: Riuniti 1980.

27. Murray, *op. cit.*, p. 75, note 6.

28. 'Piccolo e borghese', *Il Mondo*, 8 May 1981.

29. 'L'evasione IVA sfiora il 50 per cento', *Corriere della Sera*, 6 February 1980; and 'Italian taxpayers: pastassessment', *Economist*, 14 July 1984.

30. See 'Italy fights tax evasion with a new law requiring use of electronic cash registers', *Wall Street Journal*, 10 February 1983.

8. Development and under(ground) development

1. Keith Hart, 'Informal income opportunities and urban employment in Ghana', *Journal of Modern African Studies*, Vol. 11, No. 1, March 1973, p. 67. This is a revision of a paper delivered in 1971.
2. *Employment, Incomes and Equality: A Strategy for Increasing Productive Employment in Kenya*, Geneva: International Labour Office 1972, p. 5.
3. *Ibid*, p. 225.
4. S.V. Sethuraman, 'The urban informal sector: concept, measurement and policy', *International Labour Review*, Vol. 114, No. 1, July–August 1976.
5. Ray Bromley and Chris Gerry, 'Who are the casual poor?' in Bromley and Gerry (eds.), *Casual Work and Poverty in Third World Cities*, Chichester: John Wiley & Sons 1979, p. 5.
6. Chris Birkbeck, 'Garbage, industry and the "vultures" of Cali', in *ibid*, p. 182.
7. Bromley and Gerry, *op. cit.*, p. 5.
8. Alejandro Portes and John Walton, *Labor, Class and the International System*, New York: Academic Press 1981, chapter 3.
9. 'Contracting poverty', *Multinational Monitor*, August 1983.
10. See 'The instant offshore office', *Business Week*, 15 March 1982; 'Latest technology may spawn the electronic sweatshop', *New York Times*, 3 October 1982; and Ursula Huws, 'The runaway office jobs', *International Labour Reports*, March–April 1984.
11. Dimitri Germidis (ed.), *International Subcontracting: A New Form of Investment*, Paris: Organisation for Economic Co-operation and Development 1980, p. 58.
12. Rosalinda Pineda-Ofreneo, 'Philippine domestic outwork: subcontracting for export-oriented industries', *Journal of Contemporary Asia*, Vol. 12, No. 3, 1982.
13. See Enrico Paglaban, 'Philippines: workers in the export industry', *Pacific Research*, Vol. 9, No. 3–4, March–June 1978, p. 8.
14. Nestor de Oliveira, Professor of Urban and Regional Planning at Rio de Janeiro's Federal University, quoted in 'Brazil helps clandestine slum businesses go legal', *New York Times*, 9 June 1980. The Peruvian government has also taken a fairly tolerant approach to the underground economy in Peru, where one study has estimated that informal activity may equal more than 50 per cent of the official economy. See 'In Lima, even buses and clothes are part of informal economy', *Wall Street Journal*, 15 August 1984.
15. This section is based on information from the following: Peter Lupsha, 'Drug trafficking: Mexico and Colombia in comparative

perspective', *Journal of International Affairs*, Vol. 35, No. 1, Spring/Summer 1981; Roberto Junguito and Carlos Caballero, 'Illegal trade transactions and the underground economy of Colombia', in Vito Tanzi (ed.), *The Underground Economy in the United States and Abroad*, Lexington, Massachusetts: D.C. Heath 1982, and Richard Craig, 'Domestic implications of illicit Colombian drug production and trafficking', *Journal of Interamerican Studies and World Affairs*, Vol. 25, No. 3, August 1983.

16. US Congress, Senate Committee on Governmental Affairs, Permanent Subcommittee on Investigations, *Illegal Narcotics Profits*, Hearings held 7, 11, 12, 13 and 14 December 1979, Washington: Government Printing Office 1980, p. 201.

17. Craig, *op. cit.*, p. 344.

18. This section is based on information from the following: S.K. Ray, *Economics of the Black Market*, Boulder, Colorado: Westview Press 1981; and Kamal Nayan Kabra, *The Black Economy in India*, Delhi: Chanakya Publications 1982.

19. 'India's private sector: red tape, black money, white hope', *Economist*, 11 October 1980.

20. See, for example, 'Black money: quicker by underground', *Far Eastern Economic Review*, 10 November 1983.

21. Kabra, *op. cit.*, p. 46.

22. 'The black money puzzle', *Far Eastern Economic Review*, 19 October 1979.

23. They also have third-world-type informal sectors. See, for example, 'Help wanted: ear cleaner and Ganges mud seller', *New York Times*, 6 April 1984.

9. The second economy in the Soviet bloc

1. See, for example, Gregory Grossman, 'The second economy of the USSR', *Problems of Communism*, September–October 1977 and the same author's 'Notes on the illegal private economy and corruption', included in US Congress, Joint Economic Committee, *Soviet Economy in a Time of Change*, Washington: Government Printing Office 1979.

2. Hedrick Smith, *The Russians*, New York: Quadrangle Books 1976, p. 86.

3. This is the account given in Yuri Brokhin, *Hustling on Gorky Street: Sex and Crime in Russia Today*, New York: Dial Press 1975.

4. A. Katsenelinboigen, 'Coloured markets in the Soviet Union', *Soviet Studies*, Vol. 29, No. 1, January 1977.

5. Recounted in Smith, *op. cit.*, p. 96.

6. Quoted in *ibid.*, p. 86.

7. 'Living conveniently on the left', *Time*, 23 June 1980.

8. But the government is trying to crack down through the use of a computerized accounting system. See 'Soviet fights fraud with credit-card guzzler', *New York Times*, 26 March 1984.

9. Konstantin Simis, *USSR: The Corrupt Society*, New York: Simon & Schuster 1982, p. 249.

10. See 'Video's forbidden offerings alarm Moscow', *New York Times*, 22 October 1983.

11. Brokhin, *op. cit.*, Simis, *op. cit.* and Valery Chalidze, *Criminal Russia: Essays on Crime in the Soviet Union*, New York: Random House 1977.

12. See 'Russians make a big business of moonshine', *New York Times*, 8 March 1981.

13. The rest of this paragraph and the quotation are drawn from Grossman, 'Notes', *op. cit.*

14. Simis, *op. cit.*, pp. 145-6.

15. *Ibid*, pp. 149-52.

16. Cited in a survey on Hungary in the *Economist*, 20 September 1980.

17. 'Hungary takes a flier in private ownership of business enterprises', *Wall Street Journal*, 26 March 1982.

18. István Kemény, 'The unregistered economy in Hungary', *Soviet Studies*, Vol. 34, No. 3, July 1982, p. 357.

19. János Kenedi, *Do It Yourself: Hungary's Hidden Economy*, London: Pluto Press n.d., p. 99.

20. See 'Hungary takes a flier', *op. cit.* and 'Sweetening the sweat', *Economist*, 14 April 1984.

21. Ivan Volgyes, 'Hungary: socialism with a nervous tic', *Current History*, November 1982, p. 364.

22. See Andrzej Korbonski, 'The second economy in Poland', *Journal of International Affairs*, Vol. 35, No. 1, Spring/Summer 1981.

23. See 'Poland's parallel economy thriving', *New York Times*, 30 April 1983; and 'The Jaruzelski index', *Forbes*, 13 February 1984.

24. Stewart Steven, *The Poles*, New York: Macmillan 1982, p. 50.

10. Concluding notes from the underground

1. Richard Cornuelle, *Healing America*, New York: G.P. Putnam's Sons 1983, p. 143.

2. Paul Hawken, *The Next Economy*, New York: Ballantine Books 1984, p. 139.

3. The Leicester Outwork Campaign, located at 132 Regent Road in Leicester, also publishes a magazine called *Outworkers Own*.

4. See Sasha Lewis, *Slave Trade Today: American Exploitation of Illegal Aliens*, Boston: Beacon Press 1979; Tom Barry, 'On strike!

Undocumented workers in Arizona', *Southwest Economy and Society*, Vol. 3, No. 3, Spring 1978; ' "Illegals" and the courts', *NACLA Reports*, November–December 1978; and Gary Delgado, 'Organizing undocumented workers', *Social Policy*, Spring 1983.

5. Stuart Henry, 'The working unemployed: perspectives on the informal economy and unemployment', *Sociological Review*, Vol. 30, No. 3, August 1982, p. 472.

6. Dominique Desanti, 'Des travailleurs sans chaines', *Le Nouvel Observateur*, 1 October 1979, p. 68.

7. Karl Marx and Friedrich Engels, *The German Ideology*, New York: International Publishers 1947, p. 22.

Appendix

1. Raffaele De Grazia, *Clandestine Employment*, Geneva: International Labour Office 1984, pp. 13–14.

2. Technical differences between the two series also have to be taken into account. See Alexander Korns, 'Cyclical fluctuations in the difference between the payroll and household measures of employment', *Survey of Current Business*, May 1979.

3. Edward Denison, 'Is US growth understated because of the underground economy? Employment ratios suggest not', *Review of Income and Wealth*, March 1982.

4. US Congress, Joint Economic Committee, *Growth of the Underground Economy, 1950–81*, Washington: Government Printing Office 1983, pp. 7–8.

5. Denison, *op. cit.*

6. On the UK and the rest of the EEC, see Jeremy Alden and Richard Spooner, *Multiple Job Holders: An Analysis of Second Jobs in the European Community*, Luxembourg: Eurostat 1982.

7. US Congress, Joint Economic Committee, *op. cit.*, pp. 11–12.

8. See Stephen Castles, *Here for Good: Western Europe's New Ethnic Minorities*, London: Pluto Press 1984.

9. For a review of this research, see US Internal Revenue Service, *Income Tax Compliance Research: Estimates for 1973–1981*, Washington: Government Printing Office 1983, Appendix E.

10. US Congress, Select Committee on Population, *Legal and Illegal Immigration to the United States*, Washington: Government Printing Office 1978, pp. 40–41.

11. See, for example, 'Taxes aliens pay to Texas found to top benefits', *New York Times*, 15 November 1983.

12. US Internal Revenue Service, *op. cit*, p. 129.

Bibliography

General and theoretical

Dan Bawley, *The Subterranean Economy*, New York: McGraw-Hill 1982.

Raffaele De Grazia, *Clandestine Employment*, Geneva: International Labour Office 1984.

Jonathan Gershuny, *Social Innovation and the Division of Labour*, Oxford: Oxford University Press 1983.

Arnold Heertje and others, *The Black Economy*, London: Pan 1982.

Stuart Henry, 'The working unemployed: perspectives on the informal economy and unemployment', *Sociological Review*, Vol. 30, No. 3, August 1982.

Stuart Henry (ed.), *Informal Institutions: Alternative Networks in the Corporate State*, New York: St Martin's Press 1981.

Rosine Klatzmann, *Le Travail Noir*, Paris: Presses Universitaires de France 1982.

Enzo Mingione, 'Informalization, restructuring and the survival strategies of the working class', *International Journal of Urban and Regional Research*, Vol. 7, No. 3, September 1983.

US Congress, House Committee on Ways and Means, Subcommittee on Oversight, *Underground Economy*, Hearings held 16 July, 10 September, 9 and 11 October 1979, Washington: Government Printing Office 1980.

Subcontracting, sweatshops, home labor

Sheila Allen, 'Production and reproduction: the lives of women homeworkers', *Sociological Review*, Vol. 31, No. 4, November 1983.

José Alonso, 'The domestic clothing workers in the Mexican metropolis', in June Nash and María Patricia Fernández-Kelly (eds.), *Women, Men and the International Division of Labor*, Albany: State University of New York Press 1983.

Marie Brown, *Sweated Labour: A Study of Homework*, London: Low Pay Unit 1974.

Simon Crine, *The Hidden Army*, London: Low Pay Unit 1979.

Dimitri Germidis (ed.), *International Subcontracting: A New Form of Investment*, Paris: Organisation for Economic Co-operation and Development 1980.

Hardy Green and Elizabeth Weiner, 'Bringing it all back home', *In These Times*, 11–17 March 1981.

Catherine Hakim, 'Employers' use of homework, outwork and freelances', *Employment Gazette*, April 1984.

— 'Homework and outwork: national estimates from two surveys', *Employment Gazette*, January 1984.

— 'Homeworking in the London clothing industry', *Employment Gazette*, September 1982.

Barbro Hoel, 'Contemporary clothing sweatshops: Asian female labour and collective organisation', in Jackie West (ed.), *Work, Women and the Labour Market*, London: Routledge & Kegan Paul 1982.

Ursula Huws, *The New Homeworkers*, London: Low Pay Unit 1984.

— 'New technology homeworkers', *Employment Gazette*, January 1984.

Naomi Katz and David Kemnitzer, 'Fast forward: the internationalization of Silicon Valley', in Nash and Fernández-Kelly (eds.), *op. cit.*

Carla Lipsig-Mummé, 'La renaissance du travail à domicile dans les économies développées', *Sociologie du Travail*, No. 3, 1983.

Philip Mattera, 'Home computer sweatshops', *The Nation*, 2 April 1983.

Swasti Mitter and Anneke van Luijken, 'A woman's home is her factory', in Wendy Chapkis and Cynthia Enloe (eds.), *Of Common Cloth: Women in the Global Textile Industry*, Amsterdam: Transnational Institute 1983.

Rebecca Morales, 'Cold solder on a hot stove', in Jan Zimmerman (ed.), *The Technological Woman: Interfacing with Tomorrow*, New York: Praeger 1983.

New York State Department of Labor, *Report to the Governor and the Legislature on the Garment Manufacturing Industry and Industrial Homework*, February 1982.

Jack Nilles, 'Teleworking: working closer to home', *Technology Review*, April 1982.

Rosalinda Pineda-Ofreneo, 'Philippine domestic outwork: subcontracting for export-oriented industries', *Journal of Contemporary Asia*, Vol. 12, No. 3, 1982.

Jill Rubery and Frank Wilkinson, 'Outwork and segmented labour markets', in Frank Wilkinson (ed.), *The Dynamics of Labour Market Segmentation*, London: Academic Press 1981.

The measurement debate

Derek Blades, 'The hidden economy and the national accounts', *OECD Occasional Studies*, June 1982.

Carol Carson, 'The underground economy: an introduction', *Survey of Current Business*, May 1984.

David Freud, 'A guide to underground economics', *Financial Times*, 9 April 1979.

Richard McDonald, 'The underground economy and BLS statistical data', *Monthly Labor Review*, January 1984.

Michael O'Higgins, 'Aggregate measures of tax evasion', *British Tax Review*, No. 5, 1981.

Richard Porter and Amanda Bayer, 'A monetary perspective on underground economic activity in the United States', *Federal Reserve Bulletin*, March 1984.

Carl Simon and Ann Witte, *Beating the System: The Underground Economy*, Boston: Auburn House 1982.

Vito Tanzi (ed.), *The Underground Economy in the United States and Abroad*, Lexington, Massachusetts: D.C. Heath 1982.

US Internal Revenue Service, *Income Tax Compliance Research: Estimates for 1973–1981*, Washington: Government Printing Office 1983.

Illegal money flows and piracy

Richard Blum, 'Offshore money flows: a large dark number', *Journal of International Affairs*, Vol. 35, No. 1, Spring/Summer 1981.

Jonathan Fenby, *Piracy and the Public*, London: Frederick Muller 1983.

Penny Lernoux, *In Banks We Trust*, New York: Doubleday 1984.

US Congress, Senate Committee on Governmental Affairs, *Crime and Secrecy: The Use of Offshore Banks and Companies*, Washington: Government Printing Office 1983.

— *Illegal Narcotics Profits*, Hearings held 7, 11, 12, 13 and 14 December 1979, Washington: Government Printing Office 1980.

Employee theft and the fiddle

Jason Ditton, *Part-time Crime: An Ethnography of Fiddling and Pilferage*, London: Macmillan 1977.

— 'Perks, pilferage and the fiddle: the historical structure of invisible wages', *Theory and Society*, Vol. 4, No. 1, 1977.

Stuart Henry, *The Hidden Economy: The Context and Control of Borderline Crime*, London: Martin Robertson 1978.

Gerald Mars, *Cheats At Work: An Anthropology of Workplace Crime*, London: Allen & Unwin 1983.

Enterprise zones

Stuart Butler, *Enterprise Zones: Greenlining the Inner Cities*, New York:

Universe Books 1981.

William Goldsmith, 'Bringing the third world home', *Working Papers*, March–April 1982.

Philip Mattera, 'From the runaway shop to the sweatshop: enterprise zones and redevelopment of the cities', *Radical America*, Vol. 15, No. 5, September–October 1981.

John Shutt, 'Tory enterprise zones and the labour movement', *Capital and Class*, No. 23, Summer 1984.

The submerged economy in Italy

Note: the Italian literature on the underground economy is huge; a sample of titles is given in the notes to chapter 7. The following are the materials available in English.

Sebastiano Brusco, 'The Emilian model: productive decentralisation and social integration', *Cambridge Journal of Economics*, Vol. 6, No. 2, June 1982.

Bruno Contini, 'Dropping out: notes on the Italian economy', *Journal of Contemporary Studies*, Summer 1981; also in Vito Tanzi (ed.), *The Underground Economy in the United States and Abroad*, Lexington, Massachusetts: D.C. Heath 1982.

— 'Labour market segmentation and the development of the parallel economy – the Italian experience', *Oxford Economic Papers*, Vol. 33, No. 3, November 1981.

Daniela Del Boca and Francesco Forte, 'Recent empirical surveys and theoretical interpretations of the parallel economy in Italy', in Tanzi (ed.), *op. cit.*

Barbara Ellis, 'Italy's prosperous anarchy', *Forbes*, 2 April 1979.

Antonio Martino, 'Measuring Italy's underground economy', *Policy Review*, Spring 1981.

Philip Mattera, 'Small is not beautiful: decentralized production and the underground economy in Italy', *Radical America*, Vol. 14, No. 5, September–October 1980.

Fergus Murray, 'The decentralisation of production – the decline of the mass-collective worker?' *Capital and Class*, No. 19, Spring 1983.

Giovanni Solinas, 'Labour market segmentation and workers' careers: the case of the Italian knitwear industry', *Cambridge Journal of Economics*, Vol. 6, No. 3, September 1982.

Marina Valcarenghi, *Child Labour in Italy*, London: Anti-Slavery Society 1981.

Norris Willatt, 'Italy's big black economy', *Management Today*, September 1982.

The informal sector in the third world

Sarthi Acharya, 'The informal sector in developing countries – a macro viewpoint', *Journal of Contemporary Asia*, Vol. 13, No. 4, 1983.

Ray Bromley and Chris Gerry (eds.), *Casual Work and Poverty in Third World Cities*, Chichester: John Wiley & Sons 1979.

Richard Craig, 'Domestic implications of illicit Colombian drug production and trafficking', *Journal of Interamerican Studies and World Affairs*, Vol. 25, No. 3, August 1983.

Roberto Junguito and Carlos Caballero, 'Illegal trade transactions and the underground economy of Colombia', in Vito Tanzi (ed.), *The Underground Economy in the United States and Abroad*, Lexington, Massachusetts: D.C. Heath 1982.

Kamal Nayan Kabra, *The Black Economy in India*, Delhi: Chanakya Publications 1982.

Alejandro Portes and John Walton, *Labor, Class and the International System*, New York: Academic Press 1981.

S.K. Ray, *Economics of the Black Market*, Boulder, Colorado: Westview Press 1981.

S.V. Sethuraman, 'The urban informal sector: concept, measurement, and policy', *International Labour Review*, Vol. 114, No. 1, July–August 1976.

W.A. Wisser, 'India's black economy', *South*, July 1981.

The second economy of the Soviet bloc

Yuri Brokhin, *Hustling on Gorky Street: Sex and Crime in Russia Today*, New York: Dial Press 1975.

Valery Chalidze, *Criminal Russia: Essays on Crime in the Soviet Union*, New York: Random House 1977.

Gregory Grossman, 'The second economy of the USSR', *Problems of Communism*, September–October 1977; also in Vito Tanzi (ed.), *The Underground Economy in the United States and Abroad*, Lexington, Massachusetts: D.C. Heath 1982

A. Katsenelinboigen, 'Coloured Markets in the Soviet Union', *Soviet Studies*, Vol. 29, No. 1, January 1977.

István Kemény, 'The unregistered economy in Hungary', *Soviet Studies*, Vol. 34, No. 3, July 1982.

János Kenedi, *Do It Yourself: Hungary's Hidden Economy*, London: Pluto Press n.d.

Andrzej Korbonski, 'The second economy in Poland', *Journal of International Affairs*, Vol. 35, No. 1, Spring/Summer 1981.

Dennis O'Hearn, 'The second economy in consumer goods and services',

Critique, No. 15, 1981.

Konstantin Simis, *USSR: The Corrupt Society – The Secret World of Soviet Capitalism*, New York: Simon & Schuster 1982.

Hedrick Smith, *The Russians*, New York: Quadrangle 1976.

Index